PRAISE FOR *BRAND STRATEGY* IN ...

"Jay Mandel is a rare gem in the literary world. He combines a wealth of life experiences and keen marketing insights into a captivating story that engages with readers on multiple levels. His unique background—which includes his work at Mastercard—has given him an unparalleled perspective on the intricacies of human nature as well as marketing strategy."

Scott Eddy, owner of @MrScottEddy, host of *Video Globetrotter* (Lifetime), and expert in brand management and hospitality

"Jay Mandel is one of the most purposeful people I know. *Brand Strategy in Three Steps* brings his methods and drive to life. He urges us to embrace the power of questioning and disruption to create a brand that aligns with customer values and stands for social good. His three-step guide is a must-read for marketers looking to elevate their approach to branding and drive long-term success."

Mark Josephson, Cofounder and CEO of Castiron and former CEO of Bitly

"When I pick up a new book, I hope to be entertained or informed. *Brand Strategy in Three Steps* offers both. I enjoyed reading it. Jay Mandel's passion and personality shine through in a refreshingly genuine way. This is a branding book, and it's also a resource for personal growth and business strategy. Everyone will benefit from reading this book, whether you're an aspiring marketer, an early-career explorer, or a CMO."

John Penrose, CEO of Leading Indicator Systems

"The thing about today's customer is that they're more conscious and aware of what they value, who they value, and why. In this book, Mandel demonstrates how authenticity influences brand and how shared values shape more meaningful relationships with customers. It highlights the importance of acting human to reach humans."

Brian Solis, digital futurist and author of *Mindshift*

Brand Strategy in Three Steps

A Purpose-Driven Approach to Branding

Jay Mandel

KoganPage

Publisher's note

Every possible effort has been made to ensure that the information contained in this book is accurate at the time of going to press, and the publishers and authors cannot accept responsibility for any errors or omissions, however caused. No responsibility for loss or damage occasioned to any person acting, or refraining from action, as a result of the material in this publication can be accepted by the editor, the publisher or the author.

First published in Great Britain and the United States in 2023 by Kogan Page Limited

2nd Floor, 45 Gee Street
London
EC1V 3RS
United Kingdom

8 W 38th Street, Suite 902
New York, NY 10018
USA

4737/23 Ansari Road
Daryaganj
New Delhi 110002
India

www.koganpage.com

Kogan Page books are printed on paper from sustainable forests.

ISBNs

Hardback   978 1 3986 0981 5
Paperback   978 1 3986 0979 2
Ebook   978 1 3986 0980 8

British Library Cataloguing-in-Publication Data

A CIP record for this book is available from the British Library.

Library of Congress Control Number

2023013913

Typeset by Integra Software Services, Pondicherry
Print production managed by Jellyfish
Printed and bound by CPI Group (UK) Ltd, Croydon, CR0 4YY

CONTENTS

01

The Meaningful Marketing Mindset

It's time to act like a marketer

Mindset matters; words matter. Actions speak louder than words

Branding is everyone's job. Yet, as a function, some people—even those within the marketing department—don't appreciate how big of a role it can and should play in their work and how to fully participate in creating brand equity.

The best brands combine their identity (values) with their value (their promise). Their actions speak louder than words. Their products work as expected, often better. They stand behind their products, and they make the right decisions on social issues.

Here are some questions that we, as marketers, can use to determine if a brand's values and promises align: Is your company's product or services offering your consumers something new? Does your audience engage with your brand frequently?

In an era where sustainability has become paramount and consumer loyalty increasingly hard to come by, it's vital for businesses to align their brand with a purpose that goes beyond profit. Companies need to find ways to engage with their customers on a deeper level if they want to prosper in today's competitive landscape. That means embedding elements of sustainability, social responsibility, and customer experience into their marketing strategies. Purpose-driven thinking is an essential way for many brands to do this.

In recent years, businesses have become increasingly aware of the need for a meaningful purpose that goes beyond convenience and offers real social good. Harvard Business School professor Ranjay Gulati focuses on this in his book *Deep Purpose* (Harper Business, 2022), outlining the advantages of "deep purpose" over "convenient purpose" and "win-win" approaches. According to Gulati, when organizations pursue deep purpose, they are guided by an overarching mission that drives decision-making at all levels. This provides the foundation for an intentional corporate culture where everyone is committed to the brand's mission and feels motivated to perform well in service of it.

Gulati's concept can have profound implications for businesses looking to maximize success without sacrificing integrity or profitability. Organizations with deep purpose tend to be well-aligned in their goals of profitable performance and social good. This can be achieved by ensuring all stakeholders (including employees, customers, and partners) benefit from an organization's vision and mission. It also requires leaders to have a long-term vision of how the business will pursue its goals and address stakeholder needs in ways that generate value sustainably over time.

Question everything—embrace the power of questioning and disruption

If you go to a doctor when something ails you, your doctor will likely take your temperature, look at your ears and eyes, and measure your blood pressure, and ask you questions about your health before diagnosing you. Sometimes, you go to the doctor for one thing only to find that this is a symptom of another problem. Beyond helping you through something that is uncomfortable, your doctor provides a treatment plan that will help you as a whole person.

If you went to that doctor with a rash and they noticed you were having heart problems, you would want the doctor to make you aware of this, not just focus on the rash. The same thing applies to the world of marketing and branding. When a marketer is brought in to fix something—like a website—they need to get to know a brand before they can start working. This marketer will need to ask questions to gauge the brand's goals and determine the best path forward. To do this, a marketer needs to engage in an inquisitive process called "discovery."

A marketer's curiosity is valuable to the broader brand. Our jobs require curiosity. Curiosity-driven branding comes from the constant quest to comprehend oneself, an organization, a situation, a clientele, and why and how teams work together. Curiosity-driven connectivity unites people based on their inherent curiosity rather than on a definite advertising plan or ambition. Instead of constructing a sales offering for products and services, your narrative needs to draw attention and arouse interest. You need to hold your market's attention long enough to inspire them to investigate a topic further by navigating web pages or viewing videos. To do this well, we need to cultivate an emotional bond between advertisers and viewers. Curiosity-driven branding provides direct insight into the products you're selling. Still, more importantly, it sparks interest, drawing people who might have been apathetic towards your brand previously closer to your brand message.

Do you act like a marketer?

A marketing role is a job. A job has requirements that you must fulfill to get paid. A marketing mindset is instinctual. You see problems as challenges through the audience's lens. You can't help but ask questions, turn ideas into insights, and translate those insights into strategies, campaigns, and movements that matter to your audience and the world. It is part of who you are, and you will never be able to shake it. This is a gift if you choose to use it.

The concept of "acting like a marketer" came to me one day before I was teaching a marketing class at a university. My students were doing what was required, but there was a noticeable gap between the tactics and strategy. I was hoping to see inspired tools and a memorable strategy that would break through the noise. I assigned a marketing concept previously covered in class to groups and gave them a space on the chalkboard to do whatever they wanted to explain. The only criteria: "don't be boring." I asked the students to post their work on LinkedIn and other social channels and engage. It became a competition. And the most personal and vulnerable content that engaged the audience received the most attention and engagement. And these ideas spread. First, it was people in the class supporting each other. Then people in the other marketing classes, professors, and parents, including one CMO parent. Then the people that work with them. This exercise inspired these new marketers to really act like a marketer should. They were digging deeper, getting uncomfortable, finding their meaning.

Brands and people

Brands should be aiming for the long term, not just the short term. Strong brands are built slowly, deliberately, and methodically. As a brand grows, it can lead to brand recognition and positive brand association. If you want your brand to continue on a long-term path, then you need to take the time to build your brand and capitalize on the power of brand recognition and association.

A brand is not possible without its people: employees and consumers. Brands are a part of people's lives and identities. People are not interested in engaging brands unless there is substance, meaning, and reciprocity. This is often lost when the people representing the brand are not invested in it. Businesses all start with an idea, of course, but the idea in and of itself will not support a business on its own. The people need to reinforce it.

The role of the marketing team is to create incredibly vital consumer touchpoints. We have to embrace the promise and potential of marketing fully. Healthy marketing habits require more than hard skills, tools, and disjointed templates. However, the internet, social media, the educational system, and most job descriptions emphasize teaching "hard skills." You can have all the technical, analytical, and design skills, degrees, and certifications in the world. However, if there isn't a culture of mutual respect, a process to ensure seamless handoffs, a team paying attention to details, and a clear and confident message to amplify, a brand will never be able to push forward and break through. These soft skills, combined with a repeatable framework that forces you to think about the problem you are solving from your audience's perspective, will yield meaningful results.

When you act like a marketer, there is no reason you need to choose between brand and performance and there is no need for fancy labels for various pieces of the marketing mix, like "growth marketing." These extraneous phrases confuse everyone and undermine the greater contribution of marketing. Even if you're promoting your business or simply yourself, do everything you can to clarify your points and amplify the creativity and authenticity behind them.

When you act like a marketer, you can't help but explore, learn more, discover, and translate it into value. To add value, you need to have values yourself. We all have values, but they are not always documented, and many don't have them committed to memory. If your core values are gaining dust on a shelf or someplace on your computer that requires an extensive search, how true to your core can your values possibly be?

The beauty of marketing is that there are many ways to get the desired result, including tried and true methodologies that have and will continue to work for marketers. However, now is the time for marketing to change with the changing times. And this change is led by branding and the people who create meaningful brands. That's you.

"Unscripted. Vulnerable. Real." The future of media is unscripted and vulnerable

The power of unscripted media is hard to deny. It can evoke emotions, tell stories, and connect with people on a deeper level. Platforms like Twitter, Instagram, and TikTok have enabled us to express ourselves to a large audience and build relationships with others. It's remarkable how people can be so creative even when they don't have high-end equipment or tools. Creating an effective connection with consumers requires that you understand your audience and their needs. People crave these authentic connections, so it is important to take time to craft stories that are engaging without relying on gimmicks or expensive production costs. Honest storytelling through meaningful visuals, audio, and text offers the audience more than just marketing materials—it creates a bond between brand and consumer for life. It is not always necessary to invest your budget in expensive tech or A-list actors. Simple and meaningful content can be equally successful in creating a genuine connection if it resonates with your viewers.

Recently, marketers have been moving away from scripted content and fancy set designs. Instead of the old scripted content, people now value more dynamic and engaging content, giving rise to a more vulnerable or more transparent exchange of the message.

Before TikTok, my personal and professional social media profiles were glorified photo albums. Now, with TikTok, I feel comfortable displaying my three-dimensional personality. It's a virtual world that is designed to share a quirky heart, diverse interests, and humor. In my own experience, this app has allowed me not only to remember moments in life but to create things that connect to those memories. Younger generations have been creating this way for years, and companies like Google, TikTok, and Meta own the IP on their creations, personas, and profiles and how they show up in the world.

Platforms focused on creativity will remain essential to the social media landscape. Although things around us might change, authenticity and connection are values that never go out of style. The next gen of media will evolve, with the metaverse making its way into the picture. The era of scripted content running through TV is long gone. With the metaverse and the evolution of media, we all will have an incredible opportunity to connect and engage with our audience while creating experiences worth remembering and discussing.

The brands that understand this new landscape and can create meaningful connections with their audience will come out on top. They will be the ones who don't try too hard to sell something but instead focus on engaging with people and creating conversations that genuinely resonate.

Here's a challenge: The next time you think of creating a piece of content, move away from static templates and think of how you can create something truly unique that resonates with people and allows them to connect.

Grow with guidance

As a marketer, you can be over the top or extremely modest. Both options won't help you get to where you need to go. If you are over the top and too pushy, people will question whether what you are offering is genuine, authentic, and sincere. As professionals, we need to feel close to the work we put forward. The way to do this is to align our work with our interests.

How can we do this?

In this book, I will help you develop an authentic approach to branding using a three-step process: identity, intention, and implementation. The first section, "identity," will allow you to break down personal barriers and determine who you are as a person and a professional. The next section, "intention," will help you develop your identity through a process of planning and goalsetting. And with identity and intention as our foundation, we will get to a timely, relevant, sincere, and meaningful final step: "implementation." The end of this book focuses on helping you take calculated steps forward to assist in the development of your brand, whether it's already established or not.

We are well-positioned today to harness the power of marketing to create meaningful change. This book will teach you how to build more authentic businesses and prepare you to have a voice in defining the future of marketing. Marketing involves decision-making, and you can only make better decisions when you genuinely understand what you're doing and why you're doing it. This journey will start with redefining everything we've believed about marketing until now and continue to the go-to-market plan and launch. Look back, act forward; are you ready to leap?

Identity

02

Light Up Your Journey

Imagine a ship sailing without an anchor. You go where the current takes you. If you don't know where you are heading, eventually you will realize you have no direction. Some may believe that when you are in the sea, you must keep moving forward and finally find another ship or a tropical island. I don't know about you, but I'm not interested in going from one ship to another; I'm not interested in sailing aimlessly. In addition, I do not want to be a passenger on the boat of my life.

When I started as an entrepreneur, I needed to fully understand what I was trying to build, what I was selling, and why someone would buy it. And when I went to sell what I had to offer, even though I desperately needed the income, I was unable to convince myself that I was adding value, and as a result, I was unable to convince others of the same. Now, with hundreds of clients who have successfully walked through my methodology, I feel differently. I know exactly what questions to ask, what to believe, and what not to think. As a result, my work feels like something other than work. Do you allow your work to feel personal?

The baseline: What's your mindset?

Marketing is fueled by confidence, trust, and personality. Marketing as a concept is not solely focused on promoting your product or service, it is also about understanding what your audience wants and how they think. To understand your audience, you need to have empathy and a firm sense of self. In our roles, we need to address the needs of others and offer solutions to them. How can we do this for others if we don't know how to help ourselves?

For generations, strength and resilience were branded as "superhuman." CEOs, parents, politicians, and entry-level employees weren't supposed to reveal vulnerability. We were encouraged to avoid sharing personal details in professional settings. We were told that we needed to show up, no matter how we felt, and perform. But some days, it's harder to do this and luckily the world is adapting to changing ways to get our work done.

Do you have a fixed mindset or a growth mindset?

Do you think about how you respond to challenges? Did you know you can train yourself to respond to challenges productively? Many wonderful people who attend my workshops believe they need help to make meaningful changes to elevate themselves and their brands. In addition, many need more time or resources to invest in creating and implementing an effective brand strategy. I often hear the same concerns: "This goes beyond my job description," "That's someone else's job," "It will be too hard," and "How will I be able to measure my progress?"

Your attitude determines your performance and engagement in facing challenges. People with a fixed or "static" mindset have a constant view of themselves. They see their abilities as unchanging and unchangeable. Their beliefs about their capabilities are not influenced by feedback from others. People with a growth or "progressive" mindset see their abilities changing over time. They believe they can improve through effort and practice. Their beliefs about their capabilities are influenced by feedback from others and their experiences.

The terms "fixed mindset" and "growth mindset" were first coined by psychologist Carol Dweck. She has conducted extensive research on the effects of different mindsets on a person's academic achievement and life. Dweck found that people with a fixed mindset—where they believe their abilities are fixed—tend to be more resistant to failure, thus making them less likely to seek out challenges and opportunities for personal growth.

A person with a fixed mindset likes to stay in their comfort zone without exploring anything beyond their skillset. As a result, they tend to be more inflexible, wary of change, and unreceptive to new ideas.

A person with a growth mindset believes that a skill can be developed through hard work and dedication. Someone with this mindset is willing to take risks and persevere despite adversity. These individuals are open-minded, flexible, adaptable, and receptive to new ideas.

The difference between the two mindsets can be seen in how people approach learning. A person with a fixed mindset often avoids challenging tasks or situations because they fear failure. This means they may only try new things or learn new skills if forced into it. A person with a growth mindset is experimentative, agile, curious, and creative.[1] This trait is also associated with positive thinking, high productivity, and the desire to persevere despite failures.

Unlock your potential with a growth mindset

Motivation is also critical to how an individual engages with tasks or activities. There are two main types of motivation: extrinsic and intrinsic. Extrinsic motivation involves external rewards that encourage someone to engage in a behavior, such as payment for work, praise for a job well done, or avoiding punishment for failing to act. Intrinsic motivation, on the other hand, is when the activity provides its reward—in the form of personal satisfaction or enjoyment. When driven by inner incentives, individuals participate in an activity because they find it attractive and pleasing.

Activities that bring us satisfaction and joy are powered by intrinsic motivation because an internal reward system fuels them. The following are some examples of intrinsic motivation:[2]

- Studying because you enjoy gaining knowledge, not simply for good grades.
- Helping a coworker with something without expecting anything in return from them.

- Pursuing a hobby such as gardening, camping, and playing sports, for aesthetic pleasure.
- Taking extra responsibility at work to improve your skills without the intention of gaining recognition.

If you want to get your team motivated intrinsically, you need to help them find things they enjoy doing and encourage them to pursue these activities.[3] The first step is to figure out what motivates your team. Then, you can work on the things that inspire them. Understanding why people are motivated and how they're motivated is essential. It helps you know where to focus your efforts.

Extrinsic motivation—be inspired to be motivated

We are extrinsically motivated when we are not inherently inspired to perform a task because it does not bring about a sense of satisfaction. Such motivation facilitates our desire to attain a reward or avoid punishment.

Not all our work brings us joy, owing to its repetitive nature, urgency, necessity, frequency, duration, or monotony. Whether dragging ourselves to work/school every morning or on weekends, we undertake tasks that might not inherently please or satisfy us. Usually, an external force or ulterior motive drives us to complete such tasks. Rewards like money, praise, and fame drive our motivation extrinsically.

However, extrinsic motivation does not necessarily mean that we are unwilling to do something, just that we seek an external reward. For example, a person might like writing but goes the extra mile to make money by turning it into a profession. Keep in mind: offering external rewards (such as cash) for something that intrinsically rewards itself (like exercise) can lower intrinsic reward.

Some examples of extrinsic motivation are:

- Working a part-time job to make extra money while still being a student.
- Going to the office on lazy days to avoid taking a pay cut.

- Completing a task well before time to earn praise and recognition.
- Doing something you don't like to avoid public judgment.

We're social creatures who interact with our environment to satisfy ourselves and others. Yet, despite being linked to various social factors, we behave independently as individuals with individual needs and desires.

Unlock the story inside you

A good story is heard, but a great story is lived. How you tell your story builds people's perception of who you are. It also limits (or liberates) your understanding of your capability. As an experiment during the writing of this book, I asked several friends "What do you stand for?" It was surprising how hard it was for some people to answer this. I am better positioned now to answer this question than I ever was, but I still need to figure it out in its entirety. However, if I am honest with myself and you, saying what I stand for isn't enough. I suspect that you might feel the same. We need to do more.

We all strive to be successful but rarely take the time to identify and address our weaknesses. It's normal to overlook our shortcomings and focus on what we can do well. But admitting our weaknesses is an important step for personal growth, as it lets us know where we might need help or guidance. Utilizing the SWOT framework is a great way to objectively analyze each area and gain valuable insight into areas where you could benefit from development or growth.

Discover yourself with your personal SWOT

Everyone needs to take the time to look within and discover who they are—and I can help with that. SWOT is a powerful tool for understanding yourself better and unlocking more of your potential.[4] The SWOT (strengths, weaknesses, opportunities, threats) framework is beneficial for evaluating areas in your life that may require more attention or improvement. It is an analytical framework that helps diagnose and determine what to focus on.

This exercise is more complex than it may seem. Many may be tempted to say they stand for (among other things) excellence in what they do, dedication to their profession, working hard, or staying on top of things—and that's great. But, if you can see yourself differently and with curiosity, have confidence in yourself, and stretch yourself, your answers may be different.

I've included an example of my personal SWOT analysis below.

- Strengths: Curiosity, candor, constant improvement, transparency, and empowerment/coaching.
- Weaknesses: Boundaries, snap judgments.
- Opportunities: Give more, be more open to possibilities, go off the straight and narrow path, take more risks in life, do not take things personally, be consistent, listen more attentively, and practice brevity.
- Threats: Time (life goes fast, and if I do not take risks now, some opportunities will pass me by).

If you don't have goals, it is hard to make progress and grow. Opportunities come from one's openness and awareness of strengths, weaknesses, and threats. It is good to play to your strengths, but even better if you can partner with others to maximize your potential.

Thinking inclusively with an openness to change

Here is an example of how I'm taking my values and my SWOT and applying them to an endeavor that will benefit me, my students, and the world: Every time I teach a lesson to marketers, I gain a new perspective about a topic I'm teaching. For example, I was teaching a class about segmentation to students at the Fashion Institute of Technology (FIT) when I realized that the way I presented information about gender was not up to date because I was still referring to "him and her." I did not necessarily consider the fact that segmentation needs to not account primarily for the sex but also the wants, needs, and preferences of the person.

Fluid insights come from life experiences that help to inform other aspects of an individual's experience. They carry relevance no matter what stage in life you may be in or how you identify, and it is useful to understand their power. Today, more than ever, gender fluidity is a topic of conversation because traditional expectations of how individuals identify have become less binary. Everyone has something to offer. We create a more compassionate and respectful world by celebrating our differences and being inclusive of diverse ways of thinking.

More and more, gender fluidity is becoming part of our conversation as we recognize and embrace the different ways individuals express themselves. Fluid insights can occur at any stage regardless of one's gender identity. As a marketer, when you can understand and appreciate that by learning and understanding different perspectives, cultures, and identities, you can contribute to a more open-minded and inclusive world.

The first step in incorporating fluidity into your daily life is to recognize its potential benefits on a personal and professional level. Combining insights from both realms helps us better understand ourselves and refine our strategies for achieving desired goals. Furthermore, this type of awareness can improve self-confidence when approaching challenging tasks by helping us apply information we gain from our own various personal experiences or interactions with others.

Being open-minded about what aspects might prove useful across personal and professional spaces can significantly improve how quickly new ideas manifest into tangible results. In addition, shedding preconceived notions from prior experiences will leave more room for actively engaging with current circumstances while having the flexibility needed should any unexpected changes arise.

Embracing fluidity within our lives could open many doors so long as mindful consideration is given to all available options before moving forward, regardless of whether they are applicable in a home or office situation! With practice, this becomes increasingly more manageable over time.

Hard skills vs. soft skills—what are the key differences?

No two people are the same. Everyone has specific hard and soft skill characteristics that make them unique. Hard skills are knowledge-based abilities that allow us to perform specific tasks or roles effectively. Soft skills, on the other hand, refer to interpersonal traits like communication, creativity, and leadership abilities.

Hard skills refer to a person's technical know-how to effectively carry out a particular task or job role. These include qualifications such as degrees and certificates and capabilities such as programming languages or web-design-software proficiency.

Soft skills can be considered an individual's natural talents, like communication and problem-solving, which they picked up through experiences and interactions with others throughout their lives. These include adaptability, collaboration, empathy, and creativity, which help manage interpersonal relationships but can also benefit product development and marketing strategies.[5]

With a balance of hard and soft skills in your arsenal, you will be well-equipped with the qualities needed for success in life and business, no matter what challenges come your way. But equally important is a brand manager having different types of expertise, which enables you to understand customers better and create marketing, products, and experiences tailored to appeal to them.

Soft skills, value, and values—share your story with confidence

Standing firmly in your convictions will make it easier to have faith in yourself and pursue your life and career trajectory. This increases the likelihood that other individuals who share your beliefs will join you and will be pulled towards your unwavering mission.

I recently had the opportunity to reflect on my career and realized that dynamic business requires openness, curiosity, and integration of hard skills, soft skills, and vision. How do you channel openness, curiosity, and integration of hard skills, soft skills, and vision? With values! In management, value is an informal term which takes multiple forms—tangible and nontangible—which can lead to the health and wellbeing of an organization in the long run.

Values are a person's core beliefs about the world and help define how a person shows up in the world and engages with others. We all operate from our values daily. They are what we use to decide what's right and wrong. They influence how we spend our time and money. And they're the part of ourselves that we use to form meaningful connections. But, like the individuals a company employs, today's companies need to stand for something more than selling a product or service.

There is nuance to values, and not all values are created equally. People and companies can share values, but how people and companies show up and apply those values should be differentiated and memorable. For example, you can use values to understand better what your customers are passionate about, why they would purchase your product or service, and how they respond to different promotions. Understanding your audience's values gives you a powerful tool for connecting on a deeper level.

Let's take a simple word, one letter away from values—the word value. We often think about money and material things when we think of value. What does value mean to you? It could be price, convenience, service, sensory, or intellectual. Furthermore, it could be monetary, emotional, social, spiritual, environmental, etc. But what is essential in life? Is it the things that are tangible? Or is it the intangible things like relationships, family, friends, health, spirituality, community, education, creativity, love, etc.?

Value differs from values, plural. Value is inherently cheaper than values. When people think about value, terms that come to mind are price, convenience, speed, etc. This is functional value and critical to delivering what your customers need. You cannot escape functional value. If you want to make your mark, you will need to be in it with consumers and take them up the value pyramid.

Facts don't sell; value does. If you have a product that uses high-quality ingredients/components, offers more than its competitors, and comes at an affordable rate, bravo! Now, dig deeper! More is required than relying entirely on your product's functional benefits to earn loyal customers today. Your product is good, but how do you make your audience believe in it? By immersing it in values before facts.

You earn your audience's confidence in your product by creating an emotional connection with them. That's step number one; something that marketers often skip!

Telling people how good you are can only take you so far; give them something to make them stay. Maslow's Hierarchy of Needs[6] can be used to determine the needs of your customers—you can leverage the pyramid to offer something precise to your client. It's powerful how individuals can feel confident in their being once their needs are met. Ask yourself: How are you helping them with their needs? Are you fulfilling a safety or physiological requirement or helping them achieve a higher sense of belonging, love, or self-esteem? How does your product contribute to scaling their levels of self-actualization?

Speaking of value and values, let's talk about AI

It's incredible what artificial intelligence (AI) can do.

Do you want to write? There's AI for that.

Do you want to paint? There's AI for that.

Do you want to service customers? There's AI for that.

Imagine the world of marketing and social media years from now. And everything you see, right down to the last detail, has been created by AI. Some might say this is a utopian future but expecting AI to replace the human element in marketing is like expecting a computer to replace Picasso's creativity or Shakespeare's musings. It simply doesn't work![7]

The data-driven marketing of today can deliver extraordinary insights into customer behavior. Still, the real story lies in understanding how customers interact with a brand and showing that through compelling narratives. In the future, the noise of AI-driven content will be loud, and the human touch that creates unique experiences will stand out.

The human element in marketing, which takes your values and turns them into value for you and your audience, is and will always be visible, and you'll know it when you see it. So the bottom line is making AI an ally, not a replacement! Let machines do their best, and humans take charge of the creative vision. That's how you'll stand out.

Make it yours and give your customers a reason to make it theirs

By providing unique and timeless offerings infused with personal meaning and emotion, we enable individuals to express a part of themselves through their home, wardrobe, and environment. Our items help build connections between us and the world around us, inspiring creativity in everyone. We bring joy into people's lives by creating objects that honor individual moments in time and pay tribute to each person's personal experiences. Through these meaningful objects, our customers are able to reflect on their lives while also being able to share their stories with others.

Flowers are more than just a gift or decoration—they can express some of your customers' most profound emotions. As a florist, you would know how to bring out these feelings through flowers, and your responsibility is to ensure that each customer feels unique and special. By understanding the intention behind each purchase, you can craft a flower arrangement that goes beyond what nature has created and truly encapsulates the sentiment of those who buy them. Try to apply this example to what you sell, whether retail, e-commerce, a service, or a pet rock; people are buying from you because they have assigned enough value to give you the amount of money you charge.

When creating floral arrangements, one of your first steps should be understanding the customer's intentions: it could be for an anniversary celebration, a wedding proposal, to express sympathy, or to say "I love you." These occasions have different meanings and require you to think carefully about which flowers best reflect those sentiments. Understanding why your client is purchasing flowers will give you powerful insight into how they want to express themselves through this medium.

As a florist, it is up to you to create meaning in the flowers you sell, by imbuing them with specific associations based on the occasion or sentiment they are intended for. Each type of flower has its own set of traditional meanings and associations. Still, it is also important for you to think beyond the flowers when crafting floral arrangements so that they impart new significance based on what's essential to specific clients or occasions. This will help build your reputation as a creative florist who knows how to craft enhanced emotional experiences that go beyond simple bouquets made from beautiful blooms.

Every brand has values that make it unique compared with other brands in that niche. Still, it's also vital for it to establish connections between its products and those values to create successful campaigns which engage consumers in meaningful ways. As a florist brand manager, this means leveraging floral arrangements to connect your company messaging and emotion evoked by thoughtful bouquets, representing everything from hope and joy to sorrowful occasions. Your offering depends upon what each customer needs during any given moment rather than relying upon predefined meaning attached solely to varieties or colors of blossoms!

Beware: if a company leads with functional value, opportunities for differentiation will not be apparent, and it will result in product-oriented definitions of products. When you are more focused on the wants and needs of customers and connect what you do with your identity and theirs, you will have a much higher chance of inspiring.

Product focus involves demonstrating a product's quality and value as a solution to customer needs. Companies can make potential customers aware of their products to drive sales through this focus. It also allows businesses to highlight their competitive advantages over similar products in the marketplace. For example, Nike uses a product-focused approach by promoting its products (shoes or apparel) on social media platforms with impressive visuals and meaningful taglines that draw attention from consumers.

Market focus is about understanding customer needs better than anyone else and connecting those needs with your customers better than competitors ever could. This includes researching current and prospective markets to gain insights into customer behavior and pinpoint areas where companies can improve their offerings. It also allows companies to tailor their strategies towards specific needs instead of simply throwing different concepts out there, hoping something works. For instance, Netflix identifies customer preferences through its recommendation engine, which is highly customized according to viewer habits based on the genre selections they have made previously while watching Netflix, which ultimately helps them retain existing customers while attracting new ones at the same time. We will get further into this later in the book.

Trust is earned

Trust is the cornerstone of any successful relationship. Fostering relationships based on trust, honesty, and respect will help you deliver products and services apart from all others.

Marketing is an ever-evolving activity, and in the modern world, it takes more than a couple of flashy ad campaigns to truly engage and connect with your audience. For optimal results, marketing endeavors should be carefully planned with an iterative approach that considers both creative vision and evolving customer needs. Effective marketing requires planning, strategy, and time.

It's not enough to set up objectives and activities once; they need to be monitored constantly and adjusted based on market feedback and customer needs. Good marketing can draw attention and revenue when executed correctly; following an iterative approach allows marketers maximum flexibility in a rapidly changing landscape while staying true to branding identities, meaning financial rewards will come sooner rather than later. Taking the time upfront for thoughtful planning combined with continual testing using real-time data leads businesses down a path towards long-lasting success—even in times of turbulence.

Tech augments values

A good understanding of storytelling is essential to succeed in today's highly competitive digital landscape. Most brands rely solely on technical strategies such as search engine optimization (SEO) when trying to enhance their online visibility—trying to trick the algorithm with their keywords and phrases—but this won't lead anywhere unless there's interesting content backing it up too. Your story must be exciting, enjoyable, and engaging enough to make people stick around without them necessarily searching for your product or service initially. Storytelling should be combined with technical necessities such as metadata and website structures which allow easy readability to achieve maximum visibility.

One mistake many brands make is rushing into tackling SEO-related tasks before considering the content itself. Imagine a burger: even if the fresh ingredients, bun, and condiments are all great, no one will enjoy eating it if it's served on a dirty plate with crumbs. The same principle applies here: unless you have stories that capture people's attention, no matter how optimized your pages are, readers won't stick around long enough to learn about what you're offering them.

This holds particularly true for businesses in competitive markets like health and wellness or financial services; to stand out from the crowd and gain customers' attention, there must be a narrative behind it. Try talking directly to your customer by telling them powerful stories or offering helpful advice or tips on issues they care deeply about and find relevant. Being informative yet entertaining can elevate any brand's growth efforts, especially when undertaken carefully through SEO tactics designed to tell an engaging story at its core instead of focusing solely on marketing techniques themselves!

Are values enough? No!

In an age of over-the-top marketing, is it possible to craft a brand that stands out without relying on extravagant promises and grandiose statements? A no-BS brand offers a refreshing alternative to the overwhelming bombast of conventional marketing. Such products are created to make a lasting impression and bring true value to customers—providing them with something they can use.

A no-BS brand focuses on delivering solutions tailored to actual customer needs rather than promoting empty promises or flashy visuals. It seeks to provide tangible value by addressing real customer problems and offering viable long-term solutions. It eliminates the need for additional puffery or hyperbole—allowing customers to make informed decisions based on clear, honest descriptions.

Creating a no-BS brand helps you stand out from traditional marketing techniques in two key ways: authenticity and credibility.[8] By focusing on delivering tangible solutions and omitting showy visuals, your brand will come across as authentic, reliable, trustworthy, and genuine. This gives your message more weight and increases its reach, as customers will be more likely to trust what you offer.

Secondly, creating a no-BS brand helps build meaningful relationships with customers as they will come away feeling like they haven't wasted their time listening to hollow advertising jargon. By fulfilling their needs effectively, you create positive experiences, resulting in stronger loyalty in the long run. Creating meaningful connections with customers increases their loyalty, also an invaluable return investment in the long run. As such, putting thoughtful effort into developing effective solutions will ultimately benefit both parties.

Finally, crafting a successful no-BS brand means being consistent in your values. Your efforts should reflect your understanding of your audience's motivations, interests, problems, etc. These should be factored into each phase of your developing process: researching customer behaviors, gathering feedback, honing strategies, etc. Your efforts should further communicate your commitment to catering feasible solutions based on core values, adding even more credibility and trustworthiness for prospective consumers, when compared with pursuing only sales conversions at any cost.

The focus of any business should be driven by the values of trustworthiness or integrity rather than solely on gaining profit wherever possible. It is important to remember that real, happy customers are not just paying customers but also those affected positively by your products or services. Companies should prioritize the needs of their consumers above all else and gently guide them on how best their product could help them in the long run. It is worth noting here that providing a satisfactory experience once rarely leads to lasting loyalty, hence the need for constantly demonstrating good values along with great products or services.

Grow together with reciprocity

Building solid relationships with customers, partners, and other stakeholders is imperative to creating sustainable success for any business. It takes time and trust to develop meaningful connections that benefit both sides, and this can only be achieved when a company abides by the principle of mutual gain. When companies take the first step to conduct their business ethically—ensuring their actions benefit those they interact with beyond short-term gains—they are laying down a strong foundation that will result in long-term profit, higher customer acquisition rates, and productive partnerships.

Mutually beneficial relationships bring individuals and businesses together. By focusing on the strengths of reciprocal exchange, the brand creates an inspiring environment where everyone truly succeeds. Reciprocity is a way of connecting with people emotionally, and it is the future of meaningful and healthy marketing. Reciprocity marketing establishes trust, loyalty, and goodwill between the company and its customers and encourages customers to go beyond simply making a purchase—they become brand ambassadors who will help spread the word about your product or service.

Reciprocity is achieved when two parties donate goods or services to each other without the expectation of return. This exchange is not just about a single transaction; it spans a relationship wherein both parties understand that their contributions will be appreciated by one another. Customers should feel appreciated for their patronage and feel they have contributed value to your business.

Creating positive customer experiences involves showing them that you care about them; it could be something as simple as providing complimentary gifts or discounts for loyal customers. It's essential to stay personal when engaging with customers so that you can create meaningful connections with them on a deeper level.

When creating mutual value exchange opportunities, you need to ensure that both participants get something out of it. You want to create a balanced dynamic where one party is expected to give up more than the other. An example of mutual value exchange would be offering free online courses in exchange for feedback on how your products or services can be improved.

Create an environment where businesses and consumers can freely flow, allowing for honest discussions about problems, new ideas, and innovation opportunities. This open dialogue shows respect from businesses to their customers, who will appreciate being considered at every stage of decision-making—something that inspires loyalty among stakeholders while fostering lasting relationships.

Be you. Make an impression

Confidence is the cornerstone of attracting abundance in your life, which is essential whether you're an employee at a brand or the brand's only employee. You can accomplish anything when you have confidence in yourself, your gifts and talents, and your commitment to seeing it through. Even so, there's more to confidence and attaining triumph than mere belief—it takes exertion, perseverance, and a pathway of shaping aspirations into actuality. A great way to reinforce confidence is to continuously adapt, and this can be applied to your branding strategy or external messaging as well: inspired transformation.

Transformation is a nice anecdotal pitch that brands—especially in the fitness, beauty, and health spaces—often use to lure in individuals aiming for a quick win, and a before and after image often accompanies it. But here's the thing: transformation comes in different shapes and sizes! It doesn't have to be big or bold. It can be small and gradual. It doesn't have to be a 180-degree shift. Sometimes, it's the smallest of changes that can lead to remarkable outcomes.

Transformation is something that you craft; it's more than a simple transaction or purchase. It's a journey of ups and downs, highs and lows—all of which can contribute to the bigger picture. And while you are on the path of transformation for yourself and your company, remember to be yourself. The sea of sameness is less appealing than it seems. There's so much more to life than following the crowd.

Choosing to blend in and follow the same templates and tactics as everybody else, you will have a nice life, and you may never wonder what is missing. Or choose to blend out, make deliberate choices about what you stand for, and like a rainbow, radiate each of your talents and make an impression. A memorable one. Differentiating yourself is more than just being unique for the sake of being unique. It's about being authentic to yourself so that you can share your gifts with the world in a way only you can. Which will you choose?

MANIFESTING ABUNDANCE: DO WE IMAGINE THINGS THAT DON'T EXIST?

The presence of something you desire defines abundance and manifesting it pertains to living by your standards of "sufficient" until it becomes true. So, does that mean you live and spend like a millionaire, hoping it becomes valid even when you aren't one right now? Yes and no.

The concept might sound misleading at first glance by urging people to live a life they fantasize about even when they cannot afford it. But it is only a part of the entire concept of manifesting abundance.

There's plenty of abundance around us: nature, wealth, success, love, and food. These things might not belong to you now, but they can if you want. All you need to do is believe.

A plan without a strategy is just an idea, as they say. The sections below cover how you can manifest anything by customizing strategies that suit your goals, temperament, and energy.

1. Document where you are, and where you'd like to be

In 2020, one of my students attended her first Vision Board Workshop. After creating her board, she realized she needed to place it somewhere she would frequently see it. She decided to put it over her bed, so it was the first thing she saw when she woke up. A year later, as she looked at that same vision board, she realized that she had achieved many of the goals on it—plus more—throughout the pandemic.

Her board helped her realize that it isn't only manifestation that can help you accomplish your goals. The small act of just looking at the board daily served as a reminder for everything she was working towards. That one action put her goals at the top of her mind each morning, and it impacted her reality.

2. Manifest abundance through the law of attraction

The human mind is powerful enough to produce thoughts that attract similar realities. So, if you're optimistic, you're bound to come across great opportunities more often than a pessimist who looks at the world cynically. Is it because the pessimist is less deserving? No. It's just because the optimist is more open to challenges and explores the positive aspect of circumstances, unlike a pessimist who negatively receives things that come their way.

Thinking about what you don't have has two sides: you can either mope about it and ruin things or use it as a motivator to work harder and achieve it. Going by the law of attraction, you need to focus on the positive aspect of dreams to attain them instead of worrying about not living them right now or about what happened in the past.

Do you want it that bad? Think that you already have it. Then it'll motivate you to obtain it.

- Think deeply about your aspirations and what would make you truly happy. Define concrete goals of where you are today and where you want to be tomorrow, a year from now, and then in five years.

- Create a vision board and display your vision and goals in a place you look at every day.

- Be very specific on what it is you are offering and who you are serving.

- You can find contentment in making others happy, but you cannot find satisfaction in pleasing others. There's a huge difference between finding your happiness in that of others and defining your joy by the standards of others. Do not confuse the two.

- Everybody has opinions, just like you do. But do not let them deter you from achieving your goal.

- Analyze your skill set and trust your ability to accomplish something with the available resources and opportunities. Your dreams matter, so don't let anybody tell you otherwise.

- Surround yourself with people and things that align with your emotional and intellectual frequency so that they propel you towards your objectives.

- Understand that you control your life, not your friends, family, or neighbors. You are the one who will deal with the consequences of your decisions, so choose wisely.

- For abundance to manifest, you need to plant seeds every day little by little until you have achieved a steady pace towards your destination.

- Don't just rely on hope and faith! Design a process that you can consistently implement day in and day out. Whether posting content on a blog, reaching out to people who may be interested in your offering, networking with friends, or asking questions—consistently put your intention into the world.

- Look for a better future but don't be ungrateful for the present. Dissatisfaction can severely harm your mind and make you lose focus.

- Manifest the positive emotions that will come with attaining that imagined reality. Think about the excitement, fulfillment, and joy you'll experience after achieving success (that you defined for yourself), which will motivate you to keep going.

- Be patient and trust the process. You made it this far and will make it to the other side.

Endnotes

1 Sicinski, A (nd) Fixed vs. growth mindset: Which is better and why it matters?, IQ Matrix, blog.iqmatrix.com/fixed-growth-mindset (archived at https://perma.cc/GU86-5U9B)

2 Ho, L (nd), What is Motivation and How to Get Motivated, Lifehack, lifehack.org/motivation-guide-how-to-get-motivated (archived at https://perma.cc/8BVE-AEUU)

3 Evans, B (nd) Team Leads: 11 skills you need to motivate your team, friday, friday.app/p/team-lead-responsibilities (archived at https://perma.cc/TX45-MG9P)

4 Mandel, J (2017, October 5) How do you know what you want if you don't know who you are?, LinkedIn Pulse, linkedin.com/pulse/how-do-you-know-what-want-dont-who-jay-mandel/ (archived at https://perma.cc/QF5J-JXMY)

5 Wright, J (2018, February 17) The origin of soft skills, JoeJag Tech RSS, code.joejag.com/2018/the-origin-of-soft-skills.html (archived at https://perma.cc/BXL2-FKRH)

6 Maslow, A H et al (1998) *Maslow on Management*, John Wiley

7 Mandel, J (2023) You want to write? There's an AI for that… , LinkedIn, za.linkedin.com/posts/jaymandel_you-want-to-write-theres-an-ai-for-that-activity-7021329479398518784-tNU6 (archived at https://perma.cc/37BF-C4VR)

8 Raymond, M (2022, February 1) Brand discussion, phone interview

03

Your Brand

As a brand manager, you need to define your own personal standards before you can define the standards of your brand. Once you do this, you will be better equipped to apply the same principles to your brand.

Your professional brand should reflect your personal values, beliefs, goals, and aspirations. The first step to developing or enhancing your brand is to determine *who* you exactly are. You need to know where you're going to determine how to get there. So, start by asking yourself some tough questions.

- What makes you happy?
- What makes you sad?
- What do you love doing?
- What do you hate doing?
- Who do you want to become?
- How will you feel if you achieve this goal?
- What would you like to change about yourself?
- What do you believe in?
- What do you fear?
- What do you dream about?
- What do you think about most?
- What do you hope for?
- What do you stand for?

- How do you want to live your life?
- What matters most to you?

If you have an established set of core beliefs and values that you can bring with you to any organization, you will be able to align yourself with the values of almost any company. This alignment or lack thereof will help you to know what you will and won't accept from an employer. And believe me, if I were interviewing for a position where I had yet to learn who they were, what they stood for, and what they valued, it would be challenging to tell if this company, team, and culture aligned with mine.

The world around us might change, but authenticity always stays in style. Knowing who you are and what your brand stands for is essential to success in today's world. Building a solid brand identity, setting intentions that align with your core values, and implementing them through intentional actions and messaging can create a powerful connection with potential customers and foster loyalty among your existing ones. But this goes way beyond how customers will react to you. It is personal. This is your life, and you need to understand who you are to maximize your potential.

Define your brand identity

A set of clearly defined values can be used to inform all other decisions related to business and brand. The most successful people in the world have the courage to define theirs publicly, so why can't you do this privately? Don't shy away from being honest and open about the good, bad, and ugly of business. Your transparency can even be embedded into your brand identity.

Your identity sets a foundation for everything you do, whether you're contributing to a brand or running it. It explains to others who you are at the core; it determines why you do what you do and why you don't do other things. So, define your values and decide what you stand for and what principles won't be compromised. Now think about how this relates to the values of an organization you've worked for: Your brand's values need to align with those of the stakeholders of the business.

Intentions guide your brand

Setting intentions means making a promise—a pledge or commitment—to yourself and those associated with your business. Intention-setting should be an ongoing process that helps inform decisions big and small related to building your brand identity. It should be framed around purpose rather than based on material elements or recognition alone, directly linking who you are as a business to meaningful objectives which are connected back to the people affected by it (customers, employees, partners).

Implementation is about delivering experiences that fulfill your promise to a specific audience

Generating experiences goes beyond messaging; it necessitates comprehending customer needs, devising creative methods to involve them, delivering an experience that satisfies those requirements at every point of contact in their journey with the brand, and then assessing the reaction to those encounters created. From how customers deal with the service or product itself to how they feel when interacting with staff members or confronting promotional messages—each must fulfill the worth assured by the deliberately designed brand character shaped before launching anything into the marketplace.

TABLE 3.1

	You	Your brand
Identity	Who are you at the core? It determines why you do what you do and why you don't do other things.	What your brand values, and what it will and won't stand for.
Intention	The promise you will keep for yourself and others. How you will channel your identity to a purpose that serves you and connects with stakeholders.	A rallying cry for your brand. How customers will experience your brand.
Implementation	Clearly and consistently executing your promise to deliver meaning and connection with your key stakeholders.	Clearly and consistently executing your brand's promise to differentiate and connect.

A journey of exploration—is your career transactional or relational?

In 2009, I worked at Mastercard. However, at that time in my career and that point in Mastercard's history, I had a hard time seeing how I was making any contribution as an employee. I felt this way until Ajay Banga came into the company as Chief Executive Officer.

Ajay is a strong leader with clearly defined opinions about how the world works and the impression he wants to make for the company. When Ajay came on board at Mastercard, he was on a mission to teach people the difference between doing well and doing good. He focused the brand strategy on acting locally and globally. His guidance taught us to fail fast and think bigger than transactional processes. He explained branding as a narrative. Eventually, Ajay's leadership spread throughout the organization, and it became easier for my colleagues and me to stay focused and understand where we fit in the story and where the customers I was working to attract fit.

When working within any company, you must consider how you connect with the company and the people you are applying to work with. In your career, it may be frustrating if you do not necessarily consume or believe in the product; people will see right through it. I am not saying that all individuals and companies must fully buy into what you are selling and how you are selling. But specific jobs are more personal than others. For example, in marketing and advertising, a lot of the work we do is created by the marketing and advertising machine. Depending on the head of brand's leadership style, a company's leader might have little to no involvement with things like advertising campaigns. This may have worked in the past but outsourcing marketing and branding these days can have irreversible consequences.

People can tell if you are passionate about a particular industry or sector, especially when selling a product/service. However, if you do not believe in what you are selling, it is still possible for you to connect with the company's message. Showing your enthusiasm through actions and verbally stating why the company mission stands out to you during job interviews is an effective way of getting potential employers to trust that you will be able to deliver their message effectively. By doing this, companies feel confident that differences in opinion regarding concept and execution between the employer and employee can be overcome.

Let's say you work for a cookie company, and the management decides to reduce the size of the cookies while increasing the price. What if another business simultaneously charges half the price for the cookies and has better marketing that appeals to customers and tastes just as good? This new brand of cookies has as good a good shot at earning consumers' confidence as any other brand. When you lose sight of who you are and what you do best, it's only a matter of time until you'll find yourself alienated from everybody else. A newer, more innovative competitor like that other less expensive brand will swoop in and steal all your customers from you. As the seller of the popular but now smaller and more expensive cookies, you risk losing the loyalty of your consumers. They might start thinking of your brand as the "expensive cookie" brand rather than the "quality cookie" brand your team has worked hard to maintain.

Big ideas don't fit small minds

If you appreciate innovation, think freely, and wish for those around you to resonate with your creative energy, then you need to work with people with boundless imagination. Individuals committed to a relational, professional relationship respect each other and encourage the blossoming of new and unconventional ideas with long-term impact. Good listeners make good partners, and so do those who have faith in your collective effort. You don't have to worry about accountability in a relational exchange because you both acknowledge each other's skills and function with optimism.

Here are some questions to think about to see if your company, co-workers, and team have a similar mindset as you:

- **Do you have the same goal?** There could be a conflict of interest in a transactional relationship owing to a difference in ambition. Only mutual interest can bring the involved parties in sync to help them give their best.

- **What kind of relationship do they have with you?** While professionalism is a positive trait, too much can lead to inflexibility, making others uncomfortable. On the other hand, a friendlier approach does not intimidate people and brings candor and honesty in expressing ideas/opinions.

- **Do you communicate or talk?** The exchange of ideas, information, and opinions between parties in a professional relationship profoundly impacts the next course of action. Conversely, the absence of clarity in discussions can leave gaps in the progression towards goals.

- **Is your approach process-oriented or result-oriented?** Is there a balance between them? A process-oriented approach to handling work strengthens the foundation of the goals achieved, while the latter accelerates goal attainment. However, both methods have blind spots that you can easily overlook in a transactional relationship.

Making important life decisions is a daunting task, especially when the wants and desires of our parents or other close figures influence these judgments. It's essential to realize that you are responsible for your destiny and can make judgment calls that weigh all options carefully before settling on a choice that you feel best suits you. When facing obstacles, focus on overcoming them rather than worrying about gaining everyone else's approval. Furthermore, having good resources (both books and people) available that align with and understand where you're coming from can provide invaluable knowledge and insight during moments like this when trust in oneself is essential.

Taking risks can be frightening, as it often involves uncertain consequences. However, when we take the plunge and believe in ourselves, it opens up our minds to tremendous rewards and clarity about where to dedicate our attention and resources for our future endeavors. Our bold decisions allow us to discover inner strength, which makes us unstoppable with newfound ambition. Success does not come from solely taking others' advice; instead, it requires an intrinsic motivation within ourselves to pursue goals we believe are attainable no matter the difficulty. That self-belief gives us the courage to have the tenacity and perseverance to make situations better despite any opposition. Ultimately this courage leads to receiving incredible rewards that could never be attained otherwise.

Confidence and security are essential to success, as having the ability to trust yourself and your abilities will help provide clarity and direction for your actions. Without confidence or security in yourself, there may be weaknesses in your strategy that others can quickly identify. You could also become vulnerable to outside influence or criticism as you rely more on external approval or validation. Having a secure sense of self when it comes to goal setting is crucial so that you can make decisions efficiently, even if they don't match up with what someone else says should be done. A solid sense of resilience and determination will help keep you focused on achieving your goals without being distracted by seeking approval from outside sources.

Being unapologetic means having the self-assurance to stand by your beliefs, values, and actions, even in the face of criticism from others. It can also mean being honest and authentic to yourself rather than constantly seeking validation or approval from others. However, being unapologetic doesn't mean being insensitive or disrespectful to others. Holding your ground and expressing yourself in a positive, assertive way that also considers other people's feelings and perspectives is possible.

Documenting your core values (identity) will make your thoughts and ideas more evident. As a result, you may become more confident and unapologetic in your beliefs and actions. This can lead to greater self-awareness, self-assurance, and personal growth. Additionally, the more you learn about yourself, the more you want to explore and share your thoughts and ideas with others. So, are you ready? Let's keep going.

04

Your Core Values

Your brand starts with you and your contribution

The Four Agreements[1] is a book by Don Miguel Ruiz which I read many years ago and refer to often. The book traces its roots to Toltec wisdom, an influential and exceptional civilization during the pre-Columbian age. You can use the Four Agreements to help you recognize truth and eliminate useless convictions, habits, and behaviors.

Understanding the agreements allows employers to focus on developing a work culture that encourages people to speak their truth in a kind and compassionate way. This creates an atmosphere where everyone is respected and heard regardless of position or rank. This level of dialogue improves employee morale and helps employers better sympathize with their employees to understand the causes of workplace problems. By following these agreements, Ruiz believes anyone can develop self-discipline, higher awareness, inner peace, and joy. Let's dive into each agreement.

The first agreement is to be impeccable with your words. Impeccability means choosing your words and speaking consciously, honestly, respectfully, and kindly. This means refraining from making negative statements about yourself or others. When you are impeccable with your words, you practice speaking truthfully, saying what you mean, and meaning what you say.

The second agreement is not to take anything personally. This doesn't mean that you should become apathetic or emotionless, it just means that you should try not to let other people's opinions define who you are. You may encounter many things that are difficult to accept or understand, but it's important to remember that these things have nothing to do with you and shouldn't determine how you think of yourself.

The third agreement is not making assumptions about another person's intentions or believing everything they say without question. It's essential to listen carefully, ask questions if something needs to be clarified, and communicate openly so there can be a clear understanding between the two parties involved in any interaction.

And finally, the fourth agreement is always to do your best regardless of the circumstances or how difficult the situation may seem. This agreement does not require perfection, just effort, determination, and focused concentration in order to do your best.

So why would marketers and brand managers benefit from this knowledge? It's because the Four Agreements can help individuals cultivate self-awareness and inspire you and your teams with positive energy. Creating a successful brand or marketing strategy requires understanding consumer insights on thoughts and feelings towards products or services. Self-awareness helps marketers come up with creative solutions that consider all aspects of consumer needs. At times, staying confident can be difficult, especially when we experience setbacks in work projects, but having tools such as the Four Agreements allows us to maintain an optimistic mindset even during the toughest moments throughout our professional journey.

It is shocking how few people can answer the question "What do you stand for?" Not for a lack of trying; we are all so used to being told what to believe and how to behave that we don't always know who we are and what we stand for.

To optimize your personal and professional life, you must visualize your plans and place them against your current standing. What better way to define your life's direction than setting your core beliefs and promises? When you know what you stand for, you can set out your short-term and long-term objectives. You'll also be able to measure your progress towards achieving these objectives. In a later section, we'll discuss how to achieve these objectives. While this might feel like a chore initially, it has a far-reaching impact that can change how you view yourself as a person capable of balancing personal and professional aspirations. You will only know where you are heading if you assess what you can leverage in your current situation to advance your direction and what you seek to achieve.

As you think about your core beliefs, you should consider the deepest, most personal levels of changes you can make rather than focusing on the outcomes, which are simply the results of all your efforts and the processes you implement to ensure you achieve your desired results.

- **Fame:** Great! But what is fame, and why does it mean so much to you?
- **Excellence:** What do you mean by excellence, and what will you do to reach it?
- **Family:** Wonderful. I value my family too, but what words express *how* you value and empower your family?
- **Fun:** How are you fun? What does fun mean to you? Others?

If you pick an ambiguous word, you must clarify to yourself and your audience what it means and how you will apply that promise in your life.

Your identity exemplifies who you are

"Identity" involves getting to know yourself more profoundly than before. Your identity: Who are you? Moreover, who do you want to be? Knowing and understanding my identity is a vital part of life. To discover it, I need to continually learn from my experiences and evaluate what works for me, which helps me grow. As I work towards creating my authentic self, I must get out of my comfort zone, challenge myself, and take risks. Knowing who I am is beneficial because it clarifies my decisions based on my values and beliefs. Moreover, by knowing who I am, I can design a life that fulfills me and make choices aligned with my dream goals.

The future world will have a lot in common with today's world. It's not that there won't be any differences; it's just that they will be less critical and less noticeable. The world of tomorrow will be much more like today than we think. You want to start by building from your identity and then applying deliberate and purposeful actions.

Defining your identity is vital to becoming a leader and changemaker. Your identity reflects the standards that potential clients and partners expect from you, so you must understand how you want to be seen in terms of a professional brand. Defining your identity is like laying a foundation for a skyscraper. It is the fundamental starting point of self-awareness that allows you to become a leader and changemaker with an established professional brand.

Before we focus on others' desires and requirements, taking care of your own business is essential. Becoming engrossed in other people's concerns and difficulties is easy to do; however, this can manifest in confusion when trying to balance helping others while looking out for yourself, mainly if you are prone to prioritizing everyone else before yourself. If that continues, your dissatisfaction can lead to self-doubt, pressure, and even burnout—leaving you drained and no closer to acquiring what you want from life.

The key is placing yourself first. Make use of your time, take care of your wellbeing, formulate practical and accomplishable objectives, sort out obligations based on your emotional health wants, and maintain an optimistic outlook no matter the hardships encountered. Taking charge of your lifestyle will lay the groundwork even while you pursue it.

What is your identity?

Your core beliefs. I have stressed the importance of core beliefs in leading an initiative. Beliefs provide individuals with clarity of thought, allowing them to articulate their essence as a company that affects others. In addition, core beliefs come with a sense of community and motivation, enabling leaders of companies to lead with passion.

Your core beliefs also explicitly outline what type of people you wish to partner with, what type of audience you speak to, and what kind of employees you would like to hire or if you'd rather be an employer or an entrepreneur. They can also define what characteristics you stand by as a manager. While your core beliefs are an invitation for like-minded individuals, they're also disclaimers for those who disagree. Values combine a brand's purpose, the value to customers, and the impact it can make (whether that's on stakeholders or consumers—though hopefully both).

My three core values of candor, curiosity, and collaboration lay the foundation for my brand coaching role. They are at the heart of who I am as a person and serve as the basis for how I help clients to grow and learn. Becoming aware of these core values helps build my strengths and their applicability in different environments. As a brand coach, I'm passionate about bringing out the best in others by being open, curious, and collaborative. This is done through cultivating meaningful conversations, creating space for self-expression, networking with other professionals in related fields, and using resources that propel individuals towards success. As a brand coach, I am primed to inspire personal growth within myself and others daily.

But the birth of these core values was more than a one-day process. Instead, it was an iterative journey that started right from when I left corporate life, where I was deeply entrenched in the values of my company and its culture. To find my identity, I had to go through a process of digging deep into what mattered to me most and honing my skills to ensure that when I spoke or acted, it aligned with those values.

When you clearly understand your identity, you can build a brand around it and create clarity for yourself. This includes understanding your ideal audience and finding ways to connect with them. It also involves creating messaging that resonates with your core values so that when people consult you or interact with your services, they feel like a part of your story.

My core values do not merely guide me; they direct my actions. I challenge myself to continuously hone these values to ensure that whenever I interact with people, it's about creating an honest, curious, and collaborative exchange. My core values are the pillar of who I am, and they hold me accountable for what I do in my work. Even the decisions I make in my business have these three core values at their foundation.

My candor helps me understand the people I engage with and leads to more productive, transparent, and authentic relationships. This is especially important when working with clients since it's essential to creating a sense of trust to establish an effective business relationship. Additionally, my question-asking helps me identify potential problems and understand the best approach to solve them. With this value, I need to be prepared to create uncomfortable situations for myself and others, with the understanding that growth comes from discomfort.

Curiosity, on the other hand, is the drive to know more. By constantly exploring and discovering, I strive to develop new ways of creating a better experience for myself, my friends and family, my colleagues, and my clients. Curiosity also helps me stay informed on industry trends so that when I offer services and advice, it is always up to date and relevant.

Finally, collaboration brings together people I work with within an environment where they can trust one another and work towards a common goal. It's how I get teams together, develop relationships with partners, and ensure that my clients are heard.

As you can see, having core values is not just about knowing what we believe in but also understanding why they are important to us as individuals and organizations. With clear core values in place, everything else will follow. It's about taking a step back to look at who you are, what you believe in, and how you can use that to inform your decisions professionally and personally. Your core values should be the foundation of all your interactions—from customer service to daily conversations with colleagues.

But arriving at a clear set of core values is a process that takes time to develop. So instead, it's an ongoing journey that requires taking the time to reflect, look inward, and create a set of meaningful values for you. The following section explores how to go about this journey of uncovering and articulating your core values.

Let's get started with your core values

Core values provide a deeper understanding of who we are, what we want to achieve, and how to achieve it. Core values anchor our lives and allow us to remain focused on long-term fulfillment despite any distractions or obstacles that may arise in the short term. They help us understand our abilities, shape them into something meaningful, and stay aligned with our goals no matter what life throws at us. By incorporating core values into our daily lives, we can ensure that the steps taken towards success are sustainable and lead to lasting transformation. Ultimately, these core values will equip us with the tools and confidence required to put purpose ahead of pleasure and conquer any challenge.

Some people ask me if there is a right or wrong way to do a core values exercise. I would love to say there is no right or wrong way to do this, but it wouldn't be true. You will not be doing the exercise justice if your core values blend in with everyone else. If you look at the values you come up with, and it doesn't reflect who you are and what makes you unique and special compared to others, I urge you to dig deeper and get to an output that you can be proud of, that can be built on, and that defines a promise that only you can keep. You need to figure out if you're interested in looking for meaning or just looking to blend in.

Live your values

When Colonel Sanders stumbled upon the recipe for Kentucky Fried Chicken at age 65, he had no idea he would become a fast-food icon. The same can be said for Julia Child, who never cooked until she was in her 30s, or Jay Z, who didn't release his first album until he was 32. In the age of instant gratification, it's easy to think that we must have everything figured out by a certain age. However, this is far from the truth—there is always time to start something new. As a father, a coach, and a professor, I reinvent myself every year of my life, and I love the process. It's time to start living the life we want, and it's never too late.

Author and positive psychologist Emily Esfahani Smith advocates for a life of meaning over one of pure, fleeting happiness. She proposes that belonging, purpose, storytelling, and transcendence are more meaningful than feeling happy. Individuals can discover true overall satisfaction by dedicating themselves to finding purpose in life and connecting with a larger community. Meaning provides us with something genuine and tangible to strive for, making our lives more rewarding and fulfilling in the long term. Smith showcases a unique outlook on the balance between happiness and meaning; while she encourages contentment, this outlook delves deeper into the concept of creating a life well-lived.

Successful marketing requires understanding one's values and how they align with the desired dynamics of a business plan. Clarifying your values and engaging in meaningful self-examination are crucial if you want to balance reality and aspiration. All marketers need to take time for self-reflection and prioritize what's important. In this article, we will discuss why it's essential to understand yourself deeper for successful marketing.

Your values shape how you view yourself and the world around you, which is why it's essential to take time for self-reflection to ensure you are aligned with your short- and long-term business plans. Self-examination can help uncover insights into your behavior, motivations, and core beliefs so that your decisions reflect what you value most. This allows your business plan more direction when deciding between different options or strategies in marketing.

The first step to discovering your core values and how they relate to the bigger picture regarding your professional brand (be that as a consultant, company owner/founder, speaker, or employee) is going deeper into these concepts for a thorough self-examination. Here are some questions to consider:

- Who are you?
- What do you believe?
- What will you not compromise?
- How do you define happiness?

- What specific events in life gave you meaning?
  - What happened?
  - When?
  - Who was there?
  - Did you persevere?
  - If you persevered, how did you persevere?
  - What did you learn from the experience?
  - How would you do it differently if given the chance?

Take a few moments to consider the positive attributes that speak the most to you. Consider those attributes that make you most happy, give you purpose and fulfillment, and provide meaning in your life. Examples include feeling connected to nature, spending quality time with friends or family, or engaging in creative projects. Reflecting on your encounters, a few expressions or words will likely come to mind. Spend some time noting these down. Here is a set of possible terms for you to consider.

- Ambitious, Authentic
- Brave
- Candid, Curious, Collaborative
- Determined
- Empathetic, Expressive

Letting go of negative attributes can be just as crucial for success as embracing positive ones. What attributes in you and others have held you back in the past? Next, reflect on past sadness: once you have identified the positive qualities that uplift your spirit, turn your focus onto areas of past sadness. In some cases, simply reflecting on these moments may be enough—allowing old emotions to the surface so they can be released.

- What specific events in life left you feeling sad?
  - What happened?
  - When?

- o Who was there?
- o Did you persevere?
- o If you persevered, how did you persevere?
- o What did you learn from the experience?
- o How would you do it differently if given the chance?

It's also beneficial to pay attention to how various situations make you feel emotionally and cognitively—this can offer valuable insight into how specific environments may pull on deeper psychological needs or desires within yourself as a marketer. Use these reflections as clues when anything triggers internal defensiveness or negativity—this could signify that some unconscious core values are being compromised. For example, has a specific event in life ever made you feel:

- Arrogant
- Boring
- Cowardly
- Deceitful, or
- Egotistical?

Further, think about people who have succeeded in their particular field and who inspire you—what have they done differently? Why do they excel where others don't? Have they made any bold moves that propelled them further ahead than projected? Did any underlying personal values factor into those decisions along the way? Taking note of these successes can teach us not only how best approaches work but also point out our areas of potential improvement according to our individualized goals at hand—using others as examples allows us better access to thoughtful contemplation within ourselves—helping move our progress even further towards manifesting our ultimate digital dreams!

Finding core values can be a challenge, especially when crafting your own. Although Google and ChatGPT can help provide guidance, especially for easy-to-find word lists available on my website, it is essential to rely on something other than these resources verbatim. Ultimately, the success of core values lies in your ability to create an authentic set. Taking words from someone else may inspire your ideas, but they must be personal and dialed into what resonates with you and your unique perspective on abundance and success. Taking a moment to pause and reflect on what you are thankful for or the positive aspects of your life can offer perspective when addressing any sadness or negative feelings from the past.

Not only can positivity offer an opportunity for someone to heal, but it can also create change by building solid relationships, inspiring others to act and offering hope in potentially dark situations. Being conscious of our thoughts and behavior as we move through life can impact how we experience joy and peace in our present and future.

What are your top three, or even five, values? This is an amalgamation of the words you generated earlier, emphasizing where you currently stand and where you aim to be. Envision how your future will be improved and enhanced through your personal growth and development in the past. Where are you today? Where do you want to go? What do people typically anticipate from you? What surprises people about you? Who are you? What convictions do you hold dear? What will never be budged on?

Now that you have these three to five values let's "stress test" them. Can you answer these questions from your core values list?

- How would you like to be remembered?
- What is your superpower?
- What would you be doing if you didn't have to work?
- What attributes and values remain true across your personal and professional life?

Sharing a list of attributes with someone important to you can be incredibly valuable. By asking them to select the three to five words that they think best describe you, you are allowing them to consider the impact of your presence. This exercise can give you a better idea of how others think about and interpret you. Not only that, but having a friend eliminate the three words that don't talk to them about you will help narrow down the scope and focus on only those descriptors that matter most.

Be unapologetically you!

Last summer, I remembered watching a surfer as he tried to show off impossible tricks. Time and time again, he would try to show his friends something beyond his reach and fail miserably. A lot of the time, he ended up eating sand due to the amplitude and force of the wave. It was an amusing yet sad display in many ways, as it became clear that he wanted to impress more than become a better surfer. Unfortunately, the desire for perfection blinded him from the truth—that real growth is achieved through patience, dedication, and practice. I couldn't help but feel sympathy for him; here was someone who had ambition and passion but didn't know how to channel them correctly.

This fabricates an area between our actual selves and what we want them to be. We may do this out of a desire for motivated reasoning or to make ourselves look better, but these falsehoods often cause more harm than good in the long run. Whether we're at the top of our game or just beginning a journey, the idea of "You do you" is invaluable. It's the belief that success lies in genuine effort and commitment towards learning and improving your own unique set of skills—not in pretense or pretending to be something you're not.

I see many marketers and brands making the same mistake as this surfer—trying to emulate what others do and not focusing on creating something unique. "You do you" is more than just a mantra—it's a mindset. It's about understanding that success comes from building upon your strengths and pursuing authenticity instead of imitation.

On the other hand, authenticity is an uncomfortable yet courageous step towards greatness. It's about taking risks and putting yourself out there in a way no one else can.

Beware of imposter syndrome

Imposter syndrome is difficult to grapple with and can significantly impede progress in life and career. It's essential to recognize the signs of imposter syndrome, such as thoughts like "I don't measure up" or feelings of intense anxiety when faced with new challenges. To combat this feeling, it's essential to surround yourself with positive people who can provide words of encouragement and bolster your self-confidence. Challenge limiting beliefs by questioning why you think you don't belong or are not up to par; reframe those beliefs positively by focusing on successes and advancing further by acknowledging individual strengths and capabilities. Showing gratitude for accomplishments is another way to reprogram thoughts about self-worth.

Unlock a world of possibilities

Having the courage to stand out in crowded places and be true to yourself is no easy feat. It takes time to reflect on your identity and discover your core values. These values will set the foundation for developing your unique individualism and help solidify what matters to you. Taking time for self-evaluation can lead to a more profound sense of life satisfaction, making it easier to make decisions professionally and personally with confidence and clarity. Differentiating yourself allows you to express your true colors in a way that leaves an unmistakable impression. It can bolster creativity, lead others towards success, and inspire those around you. Ultimately, blending out is about taking responsibility for oneself—not just in terms of conformity but in bold self-expression that pushes boundaries and celebrates individuality.

Here are some things to consider.

- What makes your values uniquely yours?
- What is unexpected about your values? For example, a client of mine combined seemingly opposite words—soft and powerful—to deliver something that only she could.

- Are your values in the correct order? Can they build on each other?
- Should your values be looked at linearly? For example, step one, step two, step three? Or does the order not matter?
- Are specific values the foundation of who you are more than others?

Design your values

Display your values proudly. This can be a source of actualization and make decision-making easier as writing them down yields the chance to fashion something meaningful such as artwork that you can share with others. Showing your values prominently communicates how vital they are for yourself and those close to you.

There are numerous exciting means of sharing your core beliefs, such as constructing a digital resource, devising mandala artistry, making an assortment of images, or fabricating an art mobile. Take your time with the design—this is a chance to be original! You can build a billboard with photos and quotations that make it come alive. This could be through fashioning an NFT digital asset (that you can store forever online and which you would never sell, even if you become rich and famous, and it becomes "priceless"), a mandala, a collage, or even a work of art hung from the roof. Anything you go for should be remarkable and honorably showcased for everyone. Be bold with your design—this is the moment for innovation! You can visit jaymandel.com for some examples.

Above all, form sentences featuring alliteration or acronyms so that you and your audience can easily remember the essential ideas. For instance, CORE—Candid, Optimistic, Respectful, Empathetic—reminds you to act according to what is paramount for you each day. Whatever it may be, make sure you pour your uniqueness into it and make sure that it conveys what truly represents who you are!

Choose your adventure

Living your values is a critical life skill. We all have unique values, backgrounds, experiences, and dreams that can collectively shape our future outcomes. Fearlessly living our values can create transformational experiences in our personal and professional lives. Setting goals allows staying true to ourselves, developing clarity about what's essential, and taking action to impact our work, relationships, health, and overall wellbeing.

Here are some tips to help you align with your values:

Setting short-term, long-term, and mid-term goals will keep you focused throughout the year on what matters most and enable progress along the way. Goals should be SMART (specific, measurable, achievable, relevant, and timely). Include action items in each goal to ensure a process for completion. Celebrate minor victories until you reach the larger goal, which keeps the momentum moving forward! We will cover goal-setting later in the book.

Value-driven living isn't an overnight success; it's an ongoing, mentally challenging task that requires patience if you look for results that last over time. Value-driven living is best seen in those who have "walked the walk" over long periods while consistently striving to push themselves outside their comfort zone. Recognize that setbacks may occur, but don't let them deter your progress or intention. Instead, use them as learning opportunities so that they become steps towards success instead of failures.

Take responsibility for taking risks confidently when necessary, rather than hiding behind uncertainty or fleeting pleasures just for convenience's sake; this helps create new opportunities for growth within yourself and others around you.

WHEN SOMEONE HAS CORE VALUES, YOU CAN FEEL IT AND EXPERIENCE IT—THE SHAQUILLE O'NEAL STORY

Shaquille O'Neal, also known as Shaq, is a retired professional basketball player, television personality, and businessman. He is known for his larger-than-life personality and willingness to be himself, no matter what others think. From his career and public appearances, the average person can interpret and infer some core values because of the way he conducts himself. Here's an example of what his core values could look like, if he wrote them out using this method.

1 Being true to oneself: Shaq has always been unapologetically himself, and this is one of the key factors that has contributed to his success as a public figure.

2 Determination and hard work: he is known for his dedication to his craft and his willingness to work hard to achieve his goals.

3 Giving back: Shaq is known for his philanthropy and charitable work, and he has been involved in many charitable causes and has supported many non-profit organizations.

4 Relationships: he is known for his close relationships with his family and friends, and he often speaks about the importance of these relationships in his life.

5 Humor and entertainment: Shaq is known for his sense of humor and his ability to entertain others, whether it's on the basketball court or on television.

6 Entrepreneurial spirit: he is known for his business acumen and ability to identify and capitalize on opportunities to grow his brand and wealth.

When someone can see, feel, and recite your core values just from experiencing you, even if you've never explicitly told them what your core values are, it's a sign that you are genuinely living and embodying them. This means that your actions, words, and behavior are consistent with your core values and that they are a fundamental part of who you are. This consistency helps to communicate your values to others and makes them a part of your identity. When your core values are visible in your actions and behavior, it makes it easy for others to understand and relate to you, which can help to build trust and respect.

It's also worth noting that living your values can help you be more authentic, leading to greater satisfaction and fulfillment. Living your values makes you more likely to make choices that align with your beliefs and goals, which can lead to a greater sense of purpose and meaning in life.

In summary, when someone can see, feel, and recite your core values just from experiencing you, it's a sign that you are genuinely living and embodying those values, it makes you authentic and genuine to yourself, and can help to build trust and respect from others.

Endnote

1 Ruiz, M et al. (2008) *The Four Agreements: A Practical Guide to Personal Freedom.* Center Point Pub.

Intention

05

Setting Values-Based Intentions

This chapter will help you bridge the gap between your values and your customer's values.

The key to great marketing is understanding the company's and the customer's values and intentions. When a company truly understands how its customers view their needs, it can create meaningful connections that solve problems and transform the business into something extraordinary. This can be accomplished by asking your clients questions such as "What marketing problem are you trying to solve?" These conversations can lead to important insights about what strategies will best drive maximum conversions and grow a business. Additionally, it's equally important for companies to understand their own goals and resources available to develop effective solutions.

Core values are essential to getting results with any marketing campaign. Therefore, I start all my classes and most client engagements with core values. My core values are based on my personal and professional observations, insights, and experiences, which can help businesses get the most out of their campaigns. My beliefs are constantly evolving and improving based on current events and best practices to ensure clients receive the support they need to succeed in building a brand. Taking an approach that emphasizes continual improvement is critical to any successful marketing strategy.

It is important to deeply understand your brand and how you want it to be presented to customers. Your goal is for customers to connect with you, so invest time in crafting stories and messaging about who you are, your values, and why customers should trust you.

Being conscious of yourself as a product will help build trust and create authentic relationships with your customers, bringing long-term benefits beyond any initial revenue stream. Establishing the "product of you" as the foundation of future success will allow for honest communication and engage potential buyers who feel connected to the product and the person behind it.

Your intention: What do you want to become?

Good intentions in branding are essential to gain authenticity and trust with your audiences. Having a goal to reach will help you evolve further as a business and broaden your customer base. Setting positive intentions allows for collaboration among all parties involved, benefiting the customers, and creating a sustainable growth trajectory for your company.

If your expected outcome is a personal benefit, like getting a job, you need to rethink your intention! Intention can change periodically, say annually. And you keep renewing it according to the immediate goals you wish to achieve within a specific time frame. An essential takeaway from my past experiences is that one shouldn't be afraid to sell oneself. If you believe what you're offering could mean a lot to somebody, then you're doing it right. Who knows, what you think of as an interruption could keep somebody from drowning. You could be giving them a lifeboat, a life vest, or even teaching them to swim. It's a different sale for each person, but they're all equally meaningful.

And let me iterate this a little differently; changing your intention over time does not make you inauthentic! It shows that you're an evolving individual who is constantly learning and improving. It is only through newfound knowledge and experience that you rethink your existing intention to formulate a better one. Life is a series of trials and errors, and if you keep making positive amendments to your purpose, you are honest and authentic.

When approaching clients or potential customers, it's important to ensure you have an end goal or intention in mind so that everyone involved will benefit from the deal's outcome. This can also result in stronger relationships and brand loyalty by showing customers that you have their best interests at heart. And that is precisely how people connect with you. They see your failing and gaining self before placing their trust in you.

Channeling your brand ambition

Successfully generating long-term worth in life is about more than just achieving our goals; it's about having a clear vision of what we want and understanding our values, ambitions, and outlooks before designing a plan to make them a reality.[1]

Perceptions are a reality: Translating a need into an audience

How people perceive your product is how they will act on it. To the utter surprise of many, I have learned that this begins by focusing on the smallest possible audience. Making the product relevant to an audience's life helps it succeed beyond imagination. After all, one can't refuse to invest in what one relates to—a product or a service.

The best way to do this is to find the ideal audience and design your product accordingly. This means understanding your customers' needs and wants and creating products that solve those problems. It also means knowing your competition and differentiating yourself from them.

I have received many texts, books, and content from marketing gurus. Still, only the OG, Seth Godin, has created such a simple and powerful promise that forces you to make tough decisions and narrow your promise to what your audience wants and needs. He calls it the simple marketing promise.[2]

- My product is for people who believe..........
- I will focus on people who want..........
- I promise engaging with what I make will help you get..........

Here's mine:

- My product is for people curious about their full potential.
- I will focus on talented people who are open to personal and professional growth but aren't sure how.
- I promise to use my candor, experience, and network to guide you in building an action plan for your life and career.

A promise is like having a compass guiding you in the right direction. It enables you to focus on your customers' beliefs and tailor your product and service offerings to fit those beliefs. Your promise helps keep you aligned with the beliefs of your customers, so you can ensure that what they get from engaging with you reflects their values, not yours. Listening to what customers believe can help you understand how they perceive your brand and provide them with a more robust customer experience. By remaining true to the customers' beliefs, your promise is essential to finding your true north within customer relationships.

Deconstructing the simple marketing promise

My product is for people who believe...

My offering is designed for those who focus on believing what the consumers that interact with you think, not what you think. It assists in aligning yourself to what people think instead of how they perceive you. This is all about trusting in what the customers believe and not your own beliefs. It enables focusing on what people deem true instead of their emotions towards you.

I will focus on people who want...

Here, you unite your standards with what your clients look for and anticipate from you. It is important to recognize the contrast between desires and necessities. Make sure to focus on emotional benefits rather than physical or strategic benefits and convictions. At this

TABLE 5.1

	Your Brand	Your Audience
The problem		
Values		
Emotional wants		
Functional wants		
Needs		
End goal		
Timing		

point, the statement isn't about your company or business. The second half of this book uses all the concepts from the first part connected to your association or the organization in which you are employed.

I promise that engaging with what I make will help you get...

Once you figure out the requirements of your clients, make sure to cater to their needs whatever they may be. I am not merely referring to expedited delivery, excellent quality, or any of those superficial areas. Refrain from disappointing them by not coming through on what is said. Doing such is likely to procure a good standing for your brand, potentially increasing sales from loyal customers. No one desires an apathetic involvement with any product or service—clients are more likely to retain a relationship that is intimate and meets something they seek and require.

What's your movement?

Do you believe in the power of a movement? What happens when one individual decides to use their skills, passions, and knowledge to make an impact? How can they start a movement that not only makes an impact but embeds itself into our culture and communities?

Movements are powerful forces. They can spark conversation, encourage action, create accountability, challenge systems, and challenge individuals to take responsibility. How these movements come to be and what impact they have is directly related to the individual or group driving them.

There are so many causes around the world that are deserving, so you can choose to pick up any cause related to social justice, environmental protection, cultural preservation, etc. However, there is no harm in additionally focusing on small and easily manageable projects which can make a noticeable difference in our daily lives. A great example of such a movement is The Apostrophe Protection Society based in the UK, which focuses on "preserving the correct use" of one of the English language's "most abused" punctuation marks—the apostrophe. Its founder found success with this project by making even something seemingly insignificant relatively meaningful. With this unique example as inspiration, learn how to define and prioritize your movement while having a real impact on society!

Provided that you're not just a dreamer who wants to change the world but are instead willing to put in the work required to make it happen, you have an opportunity to create something meaningful for yourself and others. A movement can be a full-time job or a hobby around your day job. If you are passionate about it, you will find people who share that passion with you and help you grow; then, it can be a movement.

My movement is my company, Jay Mandel, Your Brand Coach. Your Brand Coach applies my diverse skills as a career corporate digital marketer, entrepreneur, and coach to help people understand what makes them tick and translate it into a real business or an actionable plan to connect your passion with your vocation. Seeing people receive clarity and a concrete plan from my workshops drives me to continue to evolve my movement and offerings.

There are three facets of a business that you must maintain to build a sharp brand image: identity, platform, and movement. Identity sets the foundation for having a crystal-clear vision of who you are. The platform (or channel) is the method you choose to establish your identity and share your message with your audience. It could be your website, a social media handle, or a physical presence. Once you realize and form your business identity, you must meticulously strategize how you will approach your customers on your platform. And then comes your movement, which acts as the icing on the top and enriches the customer experience. Your movement, presented as a promise, builds a deep connection with the audience. Just like identity, your personal or company's movement is also something that needs to be registered and organized by yourself. You cannot perceive your movement (or come up with one) without truly understanding who you are and how your values resonate with your customers.

Bottom line

Connecting your vision, plans, and actions with psychology helps you better understand your skills and plan of action. To understand what goes on around you, it is imperative to figure out what goes on inside your head. And most often, we need to be aware of what we truly desire and are capable of!

Undoubtedly, it is essential to rely on oneself. However, to what extent does this faith propel you? Are you making progress or lingering at the same spot? To nourish abundance entails more than merely envisioning the future—it works as a driving force that enlivens you internally each day. This shows how remarkably distinct it is from mere idle dreaming.

We addressed how imperative it is to recognize who you are and your purpose in life; your brand should mirror your idiosyncratic character and background. Nowadays, it is critical to know who you are before you can even think about understanding someone else, be it a partner, a friend, a business, a manager, or a dog. If you are unaware of who you are, then what impression do you expect to make?.[3]

We also explored the concept of intentions and how they can influence the success of a brand. Next, we will take a step back and examine why companies should care about intentions. Intentions represent the application of core values to the realities of day-to-day operations. They are the actions that make up the story of a business. To achieve this, businesses must understand the intentions behind each action and communicate them clearly to everyone involved.

Endnotes

1 Mandel, J (nd) How to write a personal mission statement (a step-by-step guide), lifehack.org/894716/how-to-write-a-personal-mission-statement (archived at https://perma.cc/8PDS-JL3B)

2 Godin, S (2019) *This is Marketing: You can't be seen until you learn to see*, Penguin Business

3 Mandel, J (2022, June 7) How to manifest abundance in all aspects of life, Lifehack, lifehack.org/895452/manifest-abundance (archived at https://perma.cc/ZVE6-RMEE)

06

Bridging the Gap

In today's highly connected and transparent business world, staying ahead of the competition requires authenticity. Gone are the days when putting on a front or "faking it till you make it" is enough to get ahead. Now is the time to be authentic, stand out in the crowd, and succeed!

The importance of being authentic has been further highlighted by platforms such as TikTok, YouTube, and Instagram, allowing viewers to connect with someone genuinely expressing themselves—allowing room for mistakes without fearing a significant backlash. As brands look more closely at engaging with customers through these channels, authenticity will become increasingly destructive if not addressed.

These demanding times require that everything is taken seriously—down to our online presence on social media. At the same time, we shouldn't allow fear of potential failure to derail us from taking risks that align with our values. As uncomfortable as it may seem, getting creative with branding initiatives can help build awareness about who you are as a business leader among your peers and establish yourself as an industry thought leader by presenting unique insights related to current industry trends while also setting yourself apart from competitors.

Are you emotionally invested in your brand?

It makes a world of difference when you are emotionally invested in what you're doing. We've all experienced this when someone does their job—they do exactly what they're supposed to do, nothing more, nothing less, but their heart and soul are not in it.

When you're emotionally invested, you feel different; you act differently because you are confident and secure. You are not invested because a company created a positive environment. You are invested because you have a feeling of pride. You feel ownership. You realize that the only thing you have is how you act and the impression you make, and that impression will be what takes you forward. It's not that hard to figure out. So, you can decide to go to work and spend all that time just collecting a paycheck if you want. In this book's early chapters, you were doing research on yourself to discover what makes you tick. Every decision you make on your values and promises encapsulates who you are and requires deep analysis. Do you think you can surprise yourself or someone you have known for 10, 15, 30, or 40 years? You bet!

To that end, recently I asked the head of content marketing at a publicly traded financial institution, "What is the heart and soul of your company?" She told me: "We have personas, a blog, and content marketing. We want to be innovative, and we want to be more accessible. We are constantly coming up with new products and connecting with consumers." When she said this, I am not sure she realized there was no mention of the unique customer they serve and the unique point of differentiation in the marketplace. Nothing she said had an ounce of heart and soul or strategy. There was no promise. No point of view. No brand.

What content do you expect to produce if you're a marketing lead and view your world through a lens that has nothing to do with your business, yourself, and the customers you serve? Understanding your market and competitors requires more than listening to carefully coached talking points. Corporate strategists discover their plans by analyzing how organizations spend their resources. Strategic planning can be uncovered by reviewing financial statements, vendor contracts, investment portfolios, and other important information.

How did we get here?

The father of modern-day propaganda, Edward Bernays, paved the way for modern branding. He established the world of PR and propaganda. He understood the power of persuasion and how it could be used to influence people. In his book *Propaganda*, he wrote about the power of advertising and how it could be manipulated to persuade consumers into buying products.

Before Bernays published his book in 1928, companies were often limited in how they marketed and sold their products and services to customers. They relied on presenting facts and figures, such as the size or range of a car, rather than focusing on techniques that would engage customers deeply. However, since then, companies with successful brands have adopted several of Bernays' principles for creating a solid brand identity.

According to Bernays, the four essential elements of creating a successful brand are to create symbols, appeal to unconscious desires, normalize behavior, and get into customers' mental space. Doing these can help capture people's attention more successfully than just providing them with information about a product's features alone. Companies should focus on developing an emotional connection with their audience so they become loyal life-long customers instead of just purchasing one-off products. This involves creating powerful visuals or stories that resonate with customers and align with their values. These can be used as branding material throughout advertising campaigns or in marketing packages delivered to new or existing customers.[1]

Fast forward to the 1950s: TV ad revenue surpassed magazine and radio advertising sales, ushering in the golden age of advertising. TV advertising didn't just give companies a better way to reach consumers, it was about giving the company a strategic personality and putting a human face to the brand. Companies soon began introducing slogans, mascots, and radio jingles to promote their brands, not just their products. The golden age of advertising wasn't about the emotional benefits of the product, it was more often about features and functionality. I call this bolt-on branding. Branding took away from the integrity of why a brand was created in the first place.

In the 1990s, television advertising revenues surpassed print media. And then came the internet. With the arrival of the World Wide Web, online advertising has become an attractive alternative to traditional methods. But unlike print ads, where readers could flip through pages without reading them, people had to click on links to get anywhere. So instead of being able to skim something, they had to spend time clicking around. That meant advertisers had to make their messages much longer because people would only read so far before hitting the back button. In addition, the length of time people spent reading any given article or blog post was shrinking. People wanted to get right to the information they needed. They no longer wanted to waste time browsing through irrelevant articles.

In recent decades there has been more and more confusion around who does what, why, and how. What is the difference between PR and marketing? The main difference between the terms is that marketing focuses on selling products, while PR focuses on maintaining the company's positive reputation. But if that is the case, why do PR people put up PESO (paid, earned, shared, owned),[2] as a leading tactic to help companies to organize marketing channels?

Marketing and communications are often considered two distinct professional disciplines, but they are more closely intertwined than you may think. Both marketing and communication professionals strive to promote an organization's products and services and desire to build customer relationships. Many differences between these two fields have to do with positioning—what internal teams or kingdoms are trying to accomplish (e.g. turf wars).

The primary distinction between marketing and communication lies in their respective focuses. Marketing strategies revolve around creating awareness for a product or service, while communication strategies involve developing relationships with consumers by connecting them to a brand or organization's message. In other words, the goal for those in marketing is usually sales; those in communications mainly seek engagement with potential customers through different channels.

When figuring out which approach is most appropriate for your business objectives, it may be advantageous to bear in mind that both marketing and communication contribute to distinct areas that work together harmoniously when incorporated into a single comprehensive strategy; leveraging both can bring about strong outcomes—ones that could gain an advantage over opponents when trying to fight within a frenzied marketplace!

Modern-day marketing

While the basic concepts behind strategic planning have existed for decades, the world has only recently begun to catch up. Thinking about marketing in a one-dimensional way is no longer going to work. The main reasons for this are complicated. They include how business schools teach strategy, how businesses operate today, and the fact that there is too much lousy strategy out there. One of the biggest problems is that people who work in organizations today often need help understanding what good strategy means.

Insincerity is another major obstacle to creative thinking and trusting relationships within the business world. Gimmicks that make audiences believe they're essential undermine initiatives' true purposes and impacts. Regardless of their intended purposes, brands must come across as something other than manipulative and focus on bringing real improvements to people's lives. Today, millions of companies do mindless marketing—rather than focusing on customer insights, they pursue the old approach that concentrates on promotions. The abundance of cheap resources doesn't help.

Marketing departments need diverse perspectives from cross-functional teams. As marketers, we must demonstrate our ability to understand different perspectives. To be successful, you need to know how your personal beliefs, intentions, and actions interact. Once you can confidently say that you can, undertake the same exercise to help your organization, the organization you're working for, or your clients' organizations.

Once upon a time, there were significant obstacles to starting and running a new business. In the not-so-distant past, starting and running a business could be ridiculously expensive due to the necessary infrastructure and technology needed to make it happen. Businesses today have many more options for getting up and running quicker than ever.

These advances are making it much easier for anyone with a good idea to create their venture and impact in their industry, without breaking the bank to do it, which is inherently more innovative than letting big companies do so!

In the "old days," people would go out of their way to show off their products. They'd put themselves forward, trying to impress customers and win their trust. Today, however, they're much more likely to hide behind a website, hoping that potential clients will find them. Whether your company sells shoes, books, or something else, it's easy to fall into the trap of relying on static rather than dynamic advertising.

To effectively market any product or service, one must know the difference between a strategy and a tactic. A strategy is an overarching plan that outlines the general direction of your business, whereas a tactical approach focuses on specific actions to achieve those goals. Recognizing and appreciating that both are equally essential to achieving success is important. Often brands assume that if they create a quality product, they will be able to promote their products effectively. They assume they will attract potential customers if they spend enough on advertising. However, branding and marketing aren't just a means to an end; they're essential to building a successful business.

Too often, companies discuss who they are, their financing, or technical problems at a level only specialists would understand. Speaking this way alienates potential customers and, consciously and subconsciously, leaves a bad taste in their mouths, risking revenue and market share losses. Marketing professionals must clearly articulate their company's voice, personality, and purpose to tell a compelling narrative that resonates across all digital touch points and drives consumer value. This may include promotional activities, such as the annual Fourth of July sale, 70 percent off, buy one get one free, Black Friday sale, etc. These promotions lack tangible, dynamic meaning; they run through the motions. As marketing professionals, we must always consider where our strategies can have the most significant impact. It would help if you were strategic when choosing which tactics to use. A blog is needed; writing boring content won't cut it. Tweeting self-serving messages is a bad idea; advertising only sometimes works. Using the platform of the month is a quick fix; it may get you some attention, but it will only last for a while.

I am writing this on Black Friday, an invented holiday that used to carry more meaning and is being bombarded by out-of-touch promotions that put the needs of the customer last and the company's needs first. Unlike the Black Friday of the past, it now seems to be a last-ditch effort to sell something people wouldn't buy at its original price. Stock up now and get your years' worth of our service. Do you know how much software, services, and products consumers purchase on Black Friday that will be used once or never? Lots. And it is human nature. We think about what we want, feel excited about a deal, and even if we don't need it, we buy it and then find something else to focus on and move on. This assumes that the product is perfect, but rarely is it. And rarely is there a good enough feedback loop to ensure that a customer's issues have been adequately addressed.

Strategize for success

I believe in the power of intelligent and strategic marketing. We can ensure long-term engagement and customer interaction by putting thought and strategy into our marketing approach.

As previously discussed, there is often confusion over the terms "strategy" and "tactics," and how they relate to each other in marketing. The key difference between strategy and tactics is that strategy is higher-level, directional, and focused on long-term goals while tactics are lower-level, actionable plans, and short-term goals.

Strategies guide managers in working towards achieving objectives while tactics are specific tools that must be implemented to achieve those objectives. Strategically minded individuals tend to think more holistically about a range of options based on managerial decisions made at every level of an organization. On the other hand, tacticians focus on acting within an existing plan, usually with little input from others outside their team or area of expertise.

In short, strategic branding focuses on the overall strategy behind developing a brand identity while tactical branding is more concerned with specific techniques to increase awareness and engage customers.

Strategic branding is concerned with creating a brand identity that connects with your audience and differentiates you from competitors. It involves research into current market trends, developing a unique value proposition, creating engaging content, setting up systems to track progress, and continuously monitoring customer feedback. Another critical aspect of strategic branding is establishing relationships with partners to ensure consistency in messaging across channels.

Tactical branding centers around various tactics to increase visibility and build relationships with potential customers. This includes content marketing, email marketing, community building, and engagement through social media platforms like Twitter, Instagram, and Facebook. Tactics include search engine optimization (SEO), influencer outreach, traditional marketing materials like posters or brochures, organizing events, or offering loyalty programs and discounts. All these activities should be designed with one goal: connecting your brand's powerful customer experiences, which will drive loyalty.

Having both strategies and tactics in place helps align businesses' vision for long-term success with the requirements of day-to-day operations. Strategic branding ensures businesses are focused on presenting themselves advantageously by understanding market trends, allowing them to adjust their approach accordingly. In contrast, tactical approaches capitalize on immediate opportunities presented by changes in customer behavior or technological developments. Both also help create trust among customers, leading to increased engagement and sales over time.

Balancing strategic branding and tactical methods will better position businesses for success for many years. When done correctly, brands should be able to create experiences that stand out from the competition—experiences that make potential customers interested not just in one product but in your entire business.

Strategy	Tactics
• Why	• How
• Planning	• Doing
• Large scale	• Smaller scale
• Difficult to copy	• Easy to copy
• Long time frame	• Short time frame

Are you thinking critically?

When I was in college, I took a class called critical thinking and another one called making decisions. At the time, I couldn't fully understand and appreciate the relevance of the classes and the role that psychology and philosophy play in creating effective marketing. In hindsight, years later, I have a much better appreciation for how critical thinking can be applied to all topics, whether at home, with your kids, partner, or friends. Critical thinking is crucial to recognize what's true and false, right and wrong, and valuable and useless. It allows us to evaluate our beliefs, actions, and behaviors. It helps us to identify biases and prejudices we may hold, and it enables us to challenge others' ideas and opinions.

To think critically, we must first understand what critical thinking is. It is not simply identifying bias but understanding the process by which we come to conclusions. This means knowing how to ask questions, gather information, analyze it, and draw conclusions. The ability to think critically is one of the most important skills we can develop because it helps us to evaluate situations better and solve problems.

The future starts now—we must use our power to create positive change and progress, but only with responsibility and caution, as with great power comes great responsibility

Through the above reasoning, let's run some behaviors companies rely on to create an identity. The more and more I experience marketing and the more and more I engage with people outside of the marketing universe, the more I realize that people don't respect marketing, understand marketing, or give credit for results. It is much more challenging to work with a person who hasn't studied marketing or engaged with marketing in the way a true marketer does. There is a significant barrier to getting someone who doesn't understand and appreciate marketing to open their mind to what we know as marketers is the right thing to do. All the things I described earlier as cheap tactics are all that much of the world knows and understands about marketing. As a marketer, it's your job to be patient, be thoughtful, and figure out a way to do the right thing, sometimes without even telling your client, who may not ever get it, what you're doing and how you're doing it. I'm not suggesting that you be dishonest, but I am suggesting that you use an iterative approach to slowly ease your unaware client into a new way of thinking. You need to use marketing, the same techniques that you would use on your end audience, to convince your clients of the merits of this work.

As we discussed, people and companies don't always look to marketing and branding to fix things that aren't considered "marketing and branding." Still, the reality is that everything that contributes to a person's views on the company's reputation is considered branding. You'll have to remember that just because someone hasn't handed you permission to do something doesn't mean you can't influence it. If you figure out how to make the project digestible and not threaten other people who feel they have ownership of the issue, you'll have a good chance of addressing it. But the question is, how do you break down the problem when there are so many ways to break down marketing?

As a kid in the 1980s, I played Nintendo. The levels were linear. You knew where you were and where you were going. And often, we figured out the game and how it worked, and then we would play it repeatedly. We had fun because we were working with the tech and stories we had at the time. And it never changed. We watched TV at night, shows like *Seinfeld*, *Friends*, and *ER*, and followed along week after week. These shows had laugh tracks and jokes that were predictable. It was safe. The news at 6 pm was a ritual; after school, I would watch *Wheel of Fortune* and *Jeopardy*. Before September 11th, Hurricane Sandy, Covid, or other disasters, there were no crises every few years that caused us to reset and recalibrate our thoughts and expectations. We got newspapers delivered to us in the morning and weren't looking for any alerts every few minutes. Conversations with people of different political persuasion were much more comfortable than today. There were also no iPads, cell phones, FaceTime, wi-fi, or internet prevalence the way there is today.

I have two children, and I have had the honor and privilege of being a professor for young adults who are establishing themselves in these times. I don't envy the adversity they have to deal with, but in many ways, the society they are growing up in is more conducive to their specialized wants and needs. As a kid, I participated in many structured activities, but they weren't as specific as today, and our schedules were less full than they are today. Therefore, we had plenty of free time. Because we had so much free time, I learned creativity, patience, and how to win a thumb war. Today, children have special-ized structured activities from morning to night, even during the summer. Camps are designed exclusively for specialties, including archery, robotics, and even magic. The ones that some children attend have multiple physicians, Peloton machines, etc. Today, the meaning of relationship-building and memory-making has changed. Physical interactions are replaced with text messaging and meme-sharing. The method of communication today has evolved to assume the form of digital images and emoticons that mimic human expression and something even more profound.

When I got older, reality TV was all the rage. It was a novel concept; the people in these shows were placed into real situations and we all ate it up. Whether it was *Survivor*, *The Bachelor*, *The Amazing Race*, or *The Real Housewives* franchise, people were hungry to see what was happening in other people's lives. But there was something in the way. Commercials. Just as the show was getting good, a commercial would come on. Many of the people who were in the shows even created their own products. But the commercialization was forced and not compelling for those who consumed the products. The idea that someone could have one sitting and watch one episode and then not binge-watch several others was not a reality. The advent of DVDs and streaming options overwhelmed us with choice. Even though more content was being created, there was an over-reliance on tricks and stunts rather than classic stories that would be told from generation to generation.

Instead of simply watching a movie, people today want to participate in what is being shown. MrBeast is a well-known YouTuber who has become famous for his creative and entertaining videos. He is known for having an interactive relationship with his audience, often featuring them in the videos he produces. He does this by allowing viewers to join him in various activities within the video or offering audience members a chance to be part of a challenge. For example, he will often include fans in skits or pranks that take place on his channel. In addition, MrBeast will occasionally allow viewers to submit their own ideas so they can be featured in one of his videos. This allows his audience to have more control over what content is featured on his channel, which helps foster an even stronger connection between himself and the people who watch him.

YouTube has come a long way and has solidified its place in social media. It is where you go for long-form videos. It is supported by advertising and allows you to pay a nominal fee not to get ads. So if you don't pay, you must sit through an ad. The ads interrupt and rarely, if ever, relate to what you are watching. And my children have less and less patience for this interruption (especially when they view it on my web browser).

I still listen to "terrestrial radio," and the idea that people still have the patience to listen to tacky commercials and jingles is comical to my children and students. The paradigm has shifted; why would a DJ be needed if I can pick what I want to listen to and when I listen to it? Why would I need a DJ if I could mix and match what I want with simple-to-use technology?

There is a fluidity in the way people are growing up today; fluidity around gender and around moving from one thing to the next, and as such, there has been an awakening in people who felt stuck in the bodies and situations they were in. Today, you can live where you want and go when you want, and everything is connected. I am writing this from an Airbnb in Upstate New York next to a crackling fire. I need nothing but my laptop because even though I am in the mountains, I made sure that fast wi-fi was on the list of amenities.

Today there is a specialized platform for everything, and the world is more transparent than ever before while at the same time less transparent. Technology has completely changed the way we interact, work, and shop. The proliferation of specialized platforms has made it easier to be transparent in business dealings, allowing buyers and sellers to have clearer conversations about their highly specialized expectations:

- Airbnb—marketplace for places to stay
- Amazon—marketplace for commercial products and services
- Etsy—marketplace for creative goods and services
- Fiverr/Upwork—marketplace for freelance work

These platforms give the consumer and the employee much more choice.

Words like "curate" take on more meaning because there is more choice, making it harder for people to know what to expect, which makes way for internet ratings and reviews and their importance in what we sell and how we sell it. People look for a five-star review to vet every decision they make. And with the prevalence of maps and apps, people can't travel to a location, even if they have gone there multiple times and know where they are going, without the assistance of their iPhone, Waze, Google Maps, or Apple Maps.

Today, big box stores are becoming increasingly prevalent and offer a standardized shopping approach that aligns with what many consumers want. However, these stores often lack certain elements, such as the personal touch of a local store, where staffers know their customers and pride themselves on providing good customer service. This personal touch, the essential connection between the business and the consumer, is something that consumers may be missing when they shop at large stores, where surveys dictate store layout and staff have minimal motivation or investment in their job.

I see much hope in TikTok as a new way of viewing content consumption. First, the content is short and compelling. Many of the TikTok videos I watch are the best parts of TV episodes I would have enjoyed watching, and the best part is that the ads I see on TikTok are contextually relevant and created in the same tone and style as the content you are watching. If an advertiser started to use tacky, context ads, they would be thrown to the curb.

But this is not just about advertising or brand building; it is about creating products and services that address the needs of a carefully defined audience. To do that, you need to know them better than they know themselves, and if you are going to be considered a specialist, you will need to walk the walk and talk the talk. You can't fake it until you make it anymore.

The other day I was watching D-Nice on TikTok, and he was mixing his mix, and his daughter came through and needed a hug, and D-Nice gave her a hug while on camera and then mixed to the next song without skipping a beat. What a magical moment where a professional can be himself and be a dad at the same time and have the audience fully appreciate and understand who he is and what he's all about.

You can subscribe to a wide variety of people who align with your interests. The granularity of experiencing life is unique to you. No one has your feed of wants, tastes, and interests; if something doesn't fit, then take it off the feed.

Companies, in many cases, have overcorrected and are now advocating for causes because everyone else is. If you want to be successful, you need to think about the future. You can't just look at what other people are doing and copy them. That's how most companies fail. Case in point: we live in the era of LGBTQIA+, Black Lives Matter, and Breast Cancer Awareness. Many of these movements have been led by people and companies not traditionally seen as allies. This is called performative allyship. The word ally is a broad term for people who support and stand up for marginalized, oppressed, or disadvantaged people. Allies can be friends, family members, coworkers, teachers, or strangers. The term ally is vital in social justice movements because it can help to create a sense of community and solidarity. Every year in June, companies change their logos to incorporate rainbows to show support for Pride without implementing meaningful changes or inclusive behaviors to their company culture. And that is antithetical to the purpose of the very movement, where companies are doing things without substance just because everyone else is doing it.

Performative allyship is not the permanent solution. Instead, it's a short-term gratifying gimmick with long-term repercussions. If your company finds itself jumping between movements without fully committing to them, it's a major red flag for this generation of consumers. This behavior insults corporate ethics of authenticity, honesty, and transparency, killing the integrity with which people try to difference. Before you change your brand colors to the pride flag in June, or pink for cancer awareness in October, or you celebrate an invented holiday, ask yourself:

- Why would the company do this?
- What exactly are we doing? (not just putting up a logo)
- Who is it helping? (be specific)
- How will it support our company's values and promise?
  - for our team?
  - for our customers?
- What will people remember after the colorful logo is taken down?
- How can our company's business be adjusted to make our support of this cause a part of our work rather than an obligatory flash-in-the-pan campaign?

Transparency is a crucial concept for businesses today and should be embraced rather than avoided at all costs. Letting customers know exactly what goes into making the product or service will show them that you have nothing to hide—this could include studies done on ingredients used in food items or testing results for new technological advancements made by the company. By giving consumers access to behind-the-scenes processes, brands enable them to make better decisions due to increased knowledge about how things were made or developed leading up release date.

It is time for people to be more honest with themselves and others regarding the news. For example, I often hear stories on the news that feature bizarre explanations such as "logistical problems," which are too vague to make any real sense. For that message to get on the news, someone in a PR department made a statement insulting their audience's intelligence. This lack of information is unacceptable and reflects badly on the company that they think the public will accept this seemingly meaningless answer. To foster trust, honesty must be practiced, and meaningful answers must be given instead of resorting to abstract terms like logistical issues. People should speak up if they notice someone giving a bogus explanation or deflection. Otherwise, there would be no accountability or transparency.

You can't just do what everyone else is doing and think it will work. The world's BS meters are so high now that you can't manufacture a message anymore. Think of McDonald's: it was established in the 1950s but it wasn't until the 1990s that kids started calling it Mickey D's—that moniker was earned and propagated organically. There was also a fast-food place called Empanada Joe's. Right out the gate, they manufactured this fake name, M Joe's. They were trying, without success, to define and propagate a brand that they didn't earn. They tried to manufacture that grassroots name and went out of business less than a year later because they tried to synthesize and inorganically create a movement that didn't exist.[3]

Finally, encouraging inclusivity within both marketing and PR teams should be at the forefront of any marketing strategy today if it isn't already—meaning having employees from different backgrounds creating marketing solutions together through collaboration often brings original insights which may have gone unnoticed otherwise if formulating plans wasn't such an inclusive group effort. We need more diverse ideas represented throughout boardrooms if we wish true innovation to exist—so do keep this in mind moving forward!

Neurodiversity is the idea that people think, learn, and perceive information differently. This has enormous implications for education, marketers, and others interacting with people in daily life. On one hand, this presents a challenge because it can be difficult to meet the needs of all learners; on the other, it is an opportunity for innovation in teaching methods and marketing. It also brings into question how marketers should be paid since their work can only sometimes be measured in terms of hours worked. Neurodiversity is vital to recognize as we offer more personalized interactions with our customers, students, or peers. We can create more effective conversations and positive outcomes by building systems that consider individual learning styles and preferences.

Ageism is a real issue for older workers returning to work in the post-pandemic era. Many employers are biased against those over 40, assuming they must be out of touch with technology and current trends or that they will cost them too much. This type of discrimination keeps many experienced, qualified people from even applying for jobs that could make good use of their skills and experience. Many "older" workers have kept up with trends, taught themselves modern technologies and methods, and remain energetic and productive contributors to whatever work they might find themselves in. Employers must look beyond age when hiring to maximize the skills available to them to get the most efficient team possible.

Create products and services by genuinely understanding customer needs and valuing their contribution to our business

In marketing, standard conventions, terms, and methods often need more thought for the people they serve. Words such as "target market," "vendor," "consumer," and "customer" are often abused and manipulated by marketers. If, as marketers, we fail to show any regard for ourselves and the people we serve, how can we ever hope to offer genuine products and services that are useful and meaningful to others? How can we ever create products and services that are truly beneficial and valuable? The profit at the cost of the clientele's exploitation is ungenuine, and business-to-customer relationships built on respect and consent hold value. Treating the customer as a mere buyer (instead of a partner who helps our business flourish) can take away from the intention of value-based marketing. Instead, trying to understand the customer with the intention of delivering on their needs is a promising trajectory to move in. Understanding your customer is not target marketing; it is when you connect with people who may be interested in your business or brand.

Build genuine, lasting relationships with your customers by connecting meaningfully with influencers whose opinion matters

Often, businesses choose the influencer-collaboration route as a short-cut to a quick following. When working with influencers, it's tempting to focus on their number of followers as a measure of their worth. After all, the more followers they have, the more people they can help us reach, right? Well, not exactly. An influencer with a massive following can help you gain some quick visibility, but there may be better partners for your brand. Instead of chasing after the influencers with the largest followings, please focus on those genuinely engaged with their audience and who share your passion for what you do.

These influencers may have fewer followers, but the ones they do have are much more likely to be interested in your brand and in helping you build meaningful connections with your audience. And that's what it's all about. Building authentic, lasting relationships with your customers. Influencers are people whose opinion matters. You're connecting with them because they are interested in or can add significant insight into your industry. Your fans are not captive; they can choose to follow you. They can join and quit as they wish and will stick around if you deliver quality content.

Join the movement—sign the Meaningful Marketer's Pledge

In today's business world, building trust is more important than ever. But trust can't be created overnight—specific steps must be taken if you want to earn the respect of your customers. Companies can demonstrate their commitment to these principles by signing the Meaningful Marketer's Pledge.

The Modern Marketer's Pledge consists of four commitments: sincerity, authenticity, transparency, and inclusivity. Put simply, this pledge is about listening to customers, communicating honestly, engaging with people from diverse backgrounds, and using data ethically.

Developing a sincere attitude is vital in earning trust from customers or potential clients. This means knowing when it's time to step up and speak out on an issue and understanding when it's time to take a step back and listen. Being able to spot meaningful trends and thoughts can help inform strategies that focus on creating relationships instead of just trying to transact with people quickly.

Authenticity is also essential in modern marketing, as brands need to be genuine. Customers are looking for products or services they genuinely believe in—not something they think was manufactured to make a quick buck. Careful messaging and presentation can help convey values that match those of the customer base while delivering a unique perspective on any given situation or challenge.

By adopting the Meaningful Marketer's Pledge, you are committing to ethical practices and showing customers you have their best interests at heart. Here's what this pledge means for businesses and how to start adapting your mindset and approach to reflect these principles.

The Meaningful Marketer's Pledge

We believe in creating meaningful customer relationships by being sincere, authentic, transparent, and inclusive.

Values: sincerity, authenticity, transparency, inclusivity.

Sincerity—Be committed to making change through meaningful action and authenticity. Stand for taking real action, not just performing allyship.

Authenticity—Make meaningful and lasting commitments with genuine intentions towards supporting marginalized communities. Standing up for what's right and creating a safe and inclusive culture isn't just a gesture, it's our responsibility.

Transparency—Be honest with yourself and with each other. Accountability and transparency should be the foundation of society, and meaningful answers should be given instead of vague explanations.

Inclusivity—Be committed to creating an inclusive environment where everyone can reach their fullest potential, regardless of their learning styles and abilities. Strive to foster mutual understanding and respect to cultivate meaningful relationships and positive outcomes.

Your signature

Visit jaymandel.com to sign the Pledge and participate in the Meaningful Marketer's movement.

Introducing the Meaningful Marketing Collective—a community where you can escape the monotony of traditional marketing and build brands that inspire transformation. By joining this collective, you will engage in meaningful conversations to promote innovation, productivity, and social change. Become an ambassador for a brand-new way of doing business. You can learn more at jaymandel.com.

Did you see what I did there?

Right before your eyes, I took all the details from chapters 1—5 and began crafting them into a meaningful movement and platform you can participate in firsthand, and then I gave you a call to action to come to my website. And you know I will be ready for you when you come to my website; I will know where you came from, I will have my servers prepared for the onslaught of traffic from book sales, and I will have a landing page where I will offer you something of value and then get you on my email list, not by coercion but by adding value. I may send you a LinkedIn request if I find your profile interesting. I will encourage you to join me on social media and other platforms to demonstrate my product clearly and consistently. You may eventually buy one of my products or services. This is the way a marketer thinks. This is how a meaningful marketer acts.

What's your company's no-BS product?

A no-BS product challenges the uninspiring and incomplete. It represents a part of people, and they see their reflection in your brand—curated with much thought. It holds a transformational power capable of changing not just your client's experience but also their mood and state of mind. A no-BS product is created to make a lasting, memorable impression for all the right reasons.

- What are you selling your clients?
- Respectful dialogue leads to better understanding. And the goal here is to bring together stakeholders who can duke it out and drive meaningful conversations to end up with unexpected brilliance.
- How do you decide who your product is for? How do you narrow your audience and make your offering specific to them?

Case in point: Wally Health

How often do you see an Instagram ad and buy the product immediately?

If somebody buys the online product moments after seeing an ad, it's either because they wanted it or because the brand's simple marketing promise spoke to them. Have you ever experienced the latter?

When Tyler Burnett began his journey as a professional in outdoor media, he was strongly influenced by a customer-centric approach to business, which had become a long-forgotten practice in the industry.

He worked out the plan with his co-founder, and their approach was received well because they listened to their audience and built on it. Their strategy was simple: talk to the people, listen to their issues, and provide solutions accordingly. The result? People began gravitating towards their business, leaving the old for the new because they were finally getting what they wanted.

What's the important takeaway here? Tyler's business took off on people's desire for and belief in change. His business, in the process, became a beacon of hope—a firebrand for transformation.

What strikes me most about a business headed towards success? In a conversation with Tyler Burnett, the co-founder of the dental care company Wally, I noted his successful strategies that align with most of what I discuss in my branding concepts.

1 **Pricing:** It's not just about affordability but also honesty. Be clear and transparent—don't bombard your customers with surprise bills.

2 **Relationship building:** A customer lies at the heart of a business, and constantly improving your customer service makes them feel valued. And it doesn't just end there; a relationship needs to be maintained after being built. A value-oriented relationship earns trust, loyalty, and commitment, without which a business fails.

3 **Empowerment:** Let your customers know that they're in control. Tyler used media to create a dashboard, giving them control over the business's types of creatives. He listened to their audience again.

"My dentist was billing me for things he wasn't doing." Let's replace the "dentist" with another service provider. How many of us have been cheated and overcharged for poor service? Plenty, I would say. If you understand and acknowledge pain points as a consumer, you can offer specialized solutions as a business. This could go the other way, too: the company could exploit customers for their needs. As a business, how you shape customer experience stems from your understanding of pain points and core values. And that will determine how people share their experiences with you with others! Is it possible to make a profit by cutting out profitable areas? The healthcare industry is one of the most lucrative industries in the United States. And given its massively expensive nature, you wouldn't think it's customer-centric, right? But is it possible to reduce patient medical costs and still make money? Yes!

It depends on your intention: if you want to make money, you have it. But if you want to create a healthy system of changing people's lives and giving them hope alongside making healthcare accessible to everybody, then you're not at a loss.

Let me be clear: a customer-centric system is self-sustaining. If you have the entrepreneurial mind to cut down on the unnecessary—and even perverse—money-making elements of a business and focus on things that matter (and make them profitable), then you can make money. But what else will you make? A system of loyal customers who return to you and send others your way.

You must have the "I don't want to be building for anyone else but my clients" attitude. Because if you put yourself first, then the money is all you'll make (and sometimes not even that)!

Is your audience your potential clientele or your ideal market? How we see our audience significantly impacts how we approach them. If you see your audience as a target—somebody to profit from—then you're never going to treat them the right way. As a brand coach, I'm sick of being seen as a target, which makes me lose faith in the business system. A refreshing change is seeing businesses care for their consumers, where they make an effort to listen to their issues and offer solutions they need instead of selling things that they "think" their audience needs. Once we shift from "selling" to "solving," we'll have cracked the code for running a successful long-term business.

If you remain rooted in your business DNA, you will stay strong as you scale growth and achieve success. If not, you'll evolve with new people with a different set of core values, and that process will continue until you've become a new brand. And if you don't evolve into a better version of your old self, that would suck big time.

Just because the marketing department is doing "the work" doesn't mean they own the values. Everyone who is part of the process needs to feel like they put their stamp on the values, and if the values are presented correctly when revealed to broader stakeholders and audiences, they will feel a sense of pride and ownership too.[4]

So, what are you waiting for?

When an opportunity presents itself, move quickly and seize it because sometimes that window will only stay open for an instant. Acting quickly increases your chances of success and can help you achieve your goals faster. So, whether at your corporate job, small business, startup, or yourself, now is the time!

Endnotes

1 Bernays, E L and Broekhuijsen, T (2019) *Propaganda*, Schrijversportaal

2 Sparrer, C (2022, November 9) Council Post: Paid, earned, shared and owned media: Making PESO work for you, *Forbes*, forbes.com/sites/forbescommunicationscouncil/2021/07/06/paid-earned-shared-and-owned-media-making-peso-work-for-you/ (archived at https://perma.cc/NT75-XKG4)

3 Mandel, J E (2022, February 1) Interview with Marc Raymond. Used with permission

4 Ibid

Implementation

07

The Meaningful Brand Plan

After you've set your identity and intentions, it's time to start implementing these. So, if you're a leader looking to build something great, don't let a little (or a lot of) uncertainty stop you. The world needs your vision and your creativity now more than ever. It's time to step up and lead by example when it matters the most. We must remember what got us here because it will get us where we want to go.

Branding takes work. It requires a lot of thought, planning, strategy, execution, and patience. But if done right, branding can create an emotional connection between you and your customers. And once you've built that relationship, they'll come back again and again because they know what they're getting. They know who you are and what you stand for. That's why brand building is so important. People are finding new ways to experience brands. Brands are increasingly infused into people's daily lives. They're more relevant to managing our days and how we feel about ourselves.

One of the biggest hurdles may be having an unclear vision. It is essential to start from the beginning, lay out what you are trying to achieve, and inspire everyone to drive towards this common goal. Marketing needs focus. Your brand needs to be precise. A clear mandate for the marketing team will ultimately serve your customer. And the marketing department needs to be realistic about what they can influence and what's out of their control. But before we dive deep, we need to focus on that external message.

A meaningful brand plan is more than just any marketing plan. This chapter was called "The Brand Document" as a placeholder.

I looked at it and said, "I am a marketer, and I have a choice. I have creativity, insight, and goals, and I will use that to create something more memorable and better understood by my audience." Companies must leverage their skills, knowledge, and experience to create a sound brand strategy that responds to customer needs. It is only through strategically understanding our past choices and growing trends that we can design something extraordinary. And if you still fear that the audit team will come after you, you can put your findings from this book's process into your corporate template.

To create a lasting impression, a meaningful brand plan should be rooted in core values, customer relationships, and market research. It is more vulnerable than an obligatory marketing plan. It has heart, soul, energy, and enthusiasm—it is alive and constantly refined based on your learning. This foundational chapter provides an overview of the components needed when constructing a meaningful brand plan. Later chapters will provide in-depth guides on team building, market research, and putting what you learn into a go-forward implementation plan and roadmap.

Where does your brand stand?

To assess the maturity of any branding project, we look at five key factors: strategy, people, project management, technical skills, and impact.

1. Strategy

Can you recite your strategy?

What is it?

What are your tactics to deliver the strategy?

When will it be completed?

2. Leadership

Who is in charge? And who will support the project?

Who is the executive sponsor of the budget?

What is the budget of the initiative?

Who will execute?

3. Operations

What are you going to do? What's your plan?

What are the processes that came out of your strategy?

When will their strategy be executed?

What is the core creative idea?

4. How will you measure impact?

Where are your objectives and key results?

How long have you been measuring?

What revenue has your brand generated this year?

5. Technology

How will technology support your strategy and plan?

Technology is merely a tool that people use to complete processes that further their organization's strategy. What is your technology to support your objectives?

If you feel unsure about a few terms or need help answering some of the questions discussed previously, there is no need to fret; that is why this book exists. We will explore each subject at length in the upcoming chapters with valuable examples and helpful prompting questions.

Let's get to it.

Your brand's maturity defines everything you do

Brands are in different stages of maturity: some in the beginning stages with limited resources and others edging towards advanced maturity. This can range from early to advanced.

Early or immature brands, just starting to establish themselves, tend to need more resources and rely mainly on their core competencies, such as an innovative product or service. Early brands often need a defined brand image, consistency across multiple channels, and an overly aggressive promotional stance. Additionally, immature brands tend to rely too much on price to attract attention and don't invest sufficiently in research and development. Early brands are also likely to be reactive to outside influence, such as customer feedback and competitors' marketing tactics, rather than proactively setting the direction for their brand.

Attributes of an emerging brand include a distinct sense of purpose and mission, an engaging and consistent visual identity, a narrative behind the brand that connects it to its customers' journeys or aspirations, and the ability to quickly create new products or services that meet changing customer needs. In addition, emerging brands rely heavily on digital marketing, developing relationships with influencers, and innovating content to engage their audience and refine brand positioning.

As companies expand and achieve success they become intermediate-level brands which focus on explicit objectives and have their operations organized. An intermediate brand is popular among a wide range of consumers. Elements such as its name, logo, story, and marketing message are established. These elements work together to create an impression of a product or company in customers' minds. Additionally, a brand can be defined by its associated qualities like trustworthiness, reliability, innovation, and emotion which evoke customer loyalty. An intermediate brand connects with its audience, which leads to tremendous success in sales and customer retention.

A mature brand has achieved a steady position within its market and commands consumer loyalty and trust; as you embark on your journey, don't forget your personal goals, who you are, and what you ultimately want to achieve because only you will look out for you in the way you can. But here's the secret. It is the key to a happy life and a fulfilling career if you can connect what drives you, motivates you, and inspires others.

The pandemic was great for the corporate world because it weeded out companies that lacked the substance needed to sustain them through turbulent times. Survival of the fittest, as they say. Brands with weak foundations and inauthentic value systems couldn't optimize themselves according to the changing times. But, on the other hand, the ones with solid roots in their identity survived the pandemic; in fact, some came out stronger than before! This happened because of a well-synced identity and intention within the organization that drove innovation. Its people relied on the company's intention and implementation strategy to turn a disadvantage to their favor. The brands that survived were the ones that successfully innovated a way to retune and deliver the company's promise to match the needs of the changing times!

Creating precise and relevant brand guidelines

Having a unified brand message is critical to being successful in the marketplace. A solid and consistent brand identity can help create an emotional connection between you and your customers and a lasting relationship that will keep them coming back. To ensure your brand stands out from the crowd, you must pull it together in a comprehensive brand document. This article will take you through some of the elements that should be included within this document.

Here is my brand guideline template; as with all templates, feel free to make it yours, which may include reordering, omitting, or adding elements. Everything you need to complete the brand guidelines will be addressed.

Your team (Chapter 8)

Putting together a team charter for a brand is an absolute necessity for constructing and supporting a powerful brand image. It clarifies the company's ambition, perspective, and shared beliefs while connecting all concerned people across the enterprise who are accountable for the brand. A carefully designed brand charter can work as a critical reference that gauges actions, leads imaginative efforts, and ensures your primary communication remains cohesive no matter where it is being extended. This document also helps guarantee that all members of the branding team stay attuned to shared goals and can act as an encouragement when challenging tasks arise. A unified outlook is essential for producing and preserving positive change.

Situation analysis and market research (Chapter 9)

A situation analysis offers a comprehensive view of the internal and external factors affecting the success of a brand. It consists of reviewing an organization's internal operations regarding corporate culture, values, and offerings and understanding external influences such as competitors, customers, and market trends. This data-driven review can inform decisions about how to improve the success of a brand in various areas by providing insight into what needs to be done to meet current objectives. In addition, through surveys and online advertising campaigns, marketers can gain valuable insights, which can then be used to create tailored situation analyses that accurately reflect their business needs. Ultimately, the goal is to find practical solutions to benefit consumers and help the company reach its goals and objectives.

Your company's values and promise, and strategy (Chapter 10)

This is the heart of your brand and explains what makes your organization's goods or services unique. It should involve data about why you do what you do and how your work gives people benefits or customers. In addition, producing a clear route for how you intend to attain prosperity with your branding strategies will ensure the utmost efficiency when administering campaigns and projects. This chapter lays the foundation for your differentiation and your plan.

In conclusion

As a marketer, you know how important it is to be organized and systematic in every project. The branding document is the ultimate reference in ensuring that organization and safety measures are taken before starting any project. You can provide assurance and flexibility when it comes to the design of your projects by having a centralized reference with all necessary regulations, directives, workspaces, and criteria neatly contained within it. With the branding document as your go-to guide for what's necessary for success, there is no more need for guesswork or worrying about making mistakes. Instead, it provides comfort and speed in completing creative projects quickly, efficiently, and, most importantly, memorably.

08

Building Your Team

Your team is the driving force behind your business, and their skills, expertise, and passion can make all the difference to achieving your goals. But putting together a team aligned with your vision and values can take time and effort. To put together the most appropriate team, you need to know the problem you are solving, starting with the hypothesis for your project. At this early stage in the game, you should write down your thoughts about where you are and what you want to achieve.

Before you can start answering questions and solving problems, you must first gain the trust of your internal stakeholders. Once you do so, you can move past being just a marketer and become a *trusted advisor* who knows how to solve problems in new and innovative ways. When you have earned your place as an invaluable member of the team is the point when you can have the most impact.

We'll also discuss the importance of buy-in and role clarity within the team and how to ensure that everyone is working towards the same goals. By the end of this chapter, you'll have all the tools you need to plan and build a team ready to tackle any challenge and help your business soar to new heights.

Leadership is like a symphony because it involves each member of an organization playing an essential part in bringing about the desired effect. In this situation, you play the role of the conductor and must guide the musicians, but it takes everyone's performance to create a prosperous and harmonious sound. Just as each musician plays a distinct role that contributes to the overall composition, leaders in any organization must be able to coordinate multiple people and roles to achieve success. Team members must have a shared vision for things to work out well. And as mentioned previously, this is precisely what the three-step process (identity, intention, and implementation) seeks to achieve: your team ceases working as separate units and instead comes together to sync as one.

I recommend a collaborative approach to work, as it enables powerful brainstorming sessions where no product or result is the creation of a single individual. Collaboration, when done efficiently, homogenizes the result while ensuring that it delivers on the brand promise with a uniform tone.

Committees can be a great way to get multiple perspectives on a project, but it's important to remember that they can also be inefficient and time-consuming. To ensure that committees are productive, it's essential to have clear objectives and expectations for the committee members. It's also vital to ensure everyone is on the same page about what needs to be accomplished and how it should be done. Additionally, it's fundamental to have a clear leader who can keep the committee focused and on track. Finally, it's essential to ensure everyone is equally allowed to contribute their ideas and opinions. By following these guidelines, committees can effectively work together on a project while still maintaining individual identity and autonomy.

As we've also discussed, people and companies don't always look to marketing and branding to fix things that aren't considered "marketing and branding." Still, the reality is that everything that contributes to a person's views on the company's reputation is considered branding. You'll have to remember that just because someone hasn't handed you permission to do something doesn't mean you can't influence the thing that needs to be addressed. If you figure out how to make the project digestible and not threaten other people who feel ownership of the issue, you'll have a good chance of addressing it.

Logistics for the planning process

Do you sometimes feel like your work projects are never-ending journeys without a final destination? Do you continually seek knowledge but lack direction for implementing it, and when you should arrive at your final goal? If so, you are not alone; many of us are in this situation. Taking the time to plan out your desired outcomes is essential.

Which is why my company, Your Brand Coach, was established. My clients, who are engaged and committed to the process and the results, perform much better. Rather than a contracted partner that completes jobs on their to-do list, I include my clients in work and give them some hands-on experience. This process brings together creativity and effort, combining the skills and thoughts of everyone involved in one central point for a unified strategy.

To start, you should make a declaration concerning the issue you need to solve. This statement or idea, called a hypothesis, can be analyzed by getting data from market research and other investigation procedures, which we will address in the next chapter. This can be done by asking questions such as:

- What is the problem? Some prompts... (be specific):
  - Are you aiming to increase brand recognition or expand into new markets?
  - How do I build a strong brand presence?
  - How can I obtain customer loyalty and trust?
  - Does brand confusion exist?
  - Does my audience understand my message?
  - How does customer experience affect a brand?
  - What are the most common branding mistakes?
  - Does my company stand out from competitors?
- Who thinks it's a problem?
- Why do they think it's a problem?
- How does this problem affect your company today?
- How does this problem affect your company's future?
- What are we trying to achieve?
- How will we know when it has been achieved?

- Who is responsible for achieving this goal?
- What resources do we need to accomplish this goal?
- How much budget do you have available for this endeavor?
- What are the expectations of when the strategy will be completed?
- When are we expected to be in the market?
- How will we create an environment that supports and builds on our work?

Working with teams to ensure clarity of mission and objectives is essential for any successful project or venture. Team members need to be clear about their roles, strengths, and responsibilities for the team to move in a unified direction. Effective communication between team members is also essential for success. All decisions should be made collaboratively, and disagreements should be worked out together so everyone feels heard and respected. With clarity of mission and good communication between team members, collaboration can help teams increase efficiency and reach their goals faster.

With a good problem statement in hand, you can use your line of thinking to conduct market research. Remember that your problem statement is merely an assumption without research. This assumption needs to be dug further into with various insiders' and outsiders' perspectives so it can be confirmed. After retrieving the data, it can be applied to determine if a particular strategy was successful and how it impacted a company's products and services. Testing hypotheses lets businesses learn what serves them best, helping them stand out better in the competitive market.

Your team

It is critical to cast your team with motivated, skilled, resourceful, and collaborative people. Everyone needs to understand and be mindful of their commitments. Furthermore, every team member must understand due dates, deliverables, and communication. These assists guarantee everybody is on the same wavelength and aiming towards the same destination. In addition, having a leader who can keep the team focused and engaged is essential. I have worked with my friend Jon Yanovsky for many years. He's my go-to person to think about projects linearly and convert some of my sometimes wild and ambitious ideas into systematic approaches that address clients' business goals. If you are aware of your shortcomings and an organization with details is not one of your strengths, find someone like Jon on your team.

In a typical corporate environment, there are many stakeholders, and having them on your side will make a significant difference in the results you achieve. Depending on how your company is organized and how large of a company you have, you will either need to find internal people in these roles to support you or hire external support for these critical tasks. Having clear boundaries and expectations between teams in an organization is key to building trust and confidence. Having clear rules, guidelines, and expectations in place can help foster collaboration within the organization to resolve any issues that may arise effectively. Additionally, having these boundaries in place can give each team the necessary leeway needed to succeed within their respective disciplines.

The first step to setting up effective boundaries and expectations is ensuring that there are open lines of communication between all departments or teams. Everyone should know who they can reach out to if they have a question related to their work or need assistance with a project. Additionally, understanding whom to turn to seek answers and advice plays an essential role in making sure everyone stays on the same page with regard to how different tasks are handled throughout the organization. Put these details in your project charter!

Even though you are intelligent and capable, doing some roles in this project is only *your* job. The stakes are too high, and the information others understand, and their perspectives, are invaluable to your project's success. Here are some of the partners you should seek out.

Legal

A lawyer's role on a branding project is to provide legal advice and protection for businesses while establishing, registering, and enforcing their brand. A lawyer ensures that trademarks are appropriately applied for, filed, and monitored. They also guide laws governing intellectual property and copyright regulations related to the project and managing contracts between the business and other parties.

Legal and marketing are two essential functions of any business, yet both teams often need help understanding each other's role in the process. Businesses need to clearly understand the responsibilities and expectations between the legal and marketing teams for decisions that respect laws, regulations, and ethical standards to be made.

The success of a business comes from having a unified team that understands each other's roles in making decisions. Unfortunately, legal professionals may not always be familiar with the complex marketing world, so there must be role clarity if both teams are expected to work together productively. This role clarity begins by setting expectations among both teams on critical areas such as risk management, compliance needs, data privacy issues, content production and publication activities, contract negotiation, etc. This will help ensure that all campaigns, activities, messages, and products comply with applicable laws while allowing marketing efforts or growth opportunities when possible.

Once you have established role clarity between your legal department and your marketing team, effective communication becomes essential for them to work together. It is also important to remember that while attorneys may take a more risk-averse approach to protect your brand from legal trouble due to certain campaigns or products, marketers must think like attorneys because they need an understanding of how laws could affect their message or product. As such, open lines of dialogue should always remain available so that issues can be discussed quickly before anything goes wrong. Additionally, preparing discussions with sufficient research about any campaign or product could help bridge the gap between law and marketing as well as allow for arrangements that make everyone happy without compromising any ethical standards set forth by either side or any applicable laws or regulations.

Marketers are responsible for staying current on laws and regulations relevant to their industry. The stakes can be high if these rules need to be understood and adhered to, so taking the time to get familiar with the legal language is critical.

Procurement

Procurement's role on a branding project is to assist in selecting vendors, negotiating contracts, and managing expenses within budget guidelines. Additionally, they are responsible for tracking and managing orders, selecting products or services that meet the requirements of the team, conducting market research to find competitive suppliers, maintaining relationships with existing suppliers, resolving delivery issues, negotiating prices, and working with accounting staff to ensure that all vendor invoices are paid promptly.

Market research

Market research teams have a critical role in brand development initiatives. Their role includes understanding the audience and conducting audience research to assess the industry trends, customer needs and preferences, competitor analysis, and any other data required for the success of the brand project through data collection and analysis. They also use research findings to inform branding strategies, such as creating attractive customer messaging.

Media

The role of the media team on a branding project is to create strategies to spread awareness of the brand through all forms of media, from traditional newspaper and radio spots to influencer campaigns and digital marketing. The team then creates content, including videos, podcasts, whitepapers, and social media messaging. Finally, they coordinate with internal teams, external advertising firms, and relevant influencers to ensure the brand's message reaches its intended audiences.

Design

Design plays a critical role in branding projects. A brand must have a distinct visual identity that sets it apart from competitors; design helps create that. Design should be used to create logos, websites, product packaging, advertising campaigns—anything that tells customers who you are and why they should choose you over the competition. The design also communicates values and feelings—luxury or friendliness—which helps build relationships with ideal customers.

Digital

I can't believe there is still a department called digital because everything is digital these days. Nevertheless, the digital team plays a key role in the branding project, as they are responsible for developing, executing, and managing all digital plans. This includes creating content for websites and social media, monitoring analytics, managing paid search campaigns, conducting optimization experiments, optimizing for search engine visibility, and other online advertising campaigns to drive brand awareness and engagement.

Analytics

The analytics team plays an essential role in a branding project by collecting, analyzing, and interpreting data related to marketing activities. Their input helps to craft creative strategies for targeting audiences, developing communications plans, and measuring results that can influence the campaign's success. The insights from their work can shape more effective brand messages, identify new opportunities for customer engagement, inform decisions on how best to use resources, and ultimately help build better long-term relationships with customers.

Technology

The tech team plays a vital role by providing technical solutions to help realize the project goals. Their responsibilities may include developing web platforms and applications, integrating content into existing infrastructure, and designing interactive experiences for customers. They may also provide support in areas such as data analysis, analytics, user interface design, and artificial intelligence.

A tech team should *never lead* a marketing project: these need to be led by someone who understands how to speak to different audiences and develop strategies to generate interest in a product or service. Tech teams are better suited for developing the actual technology behind a marketing campaign and do not possess the same insight into consumer trends, audience preferences, and effective promotional techniques.

Working with an agency for a branding project is important because they can bring experience and insight that would be hard to achieve with internal resources. Agencies can provide strategic advice, create comprehensive campaigns, and handle design and execution, so the branding process goes smoothly. Since the success of a brand depends on consistency across media platforms, an agency can help ensure that message clarity is maintained throughout each platform.

Agencies

There is something to be said for bringing an external expert to a meeting with an executive for an interview. Even if you, the internal employee, know more about your company and how it works than the external expert, they can get more information by asking the right questions. You might feel dumb asking someone you know.

Since an agency will likely play a significant role in your branding project, we will detail how you can and should work with an agency partner. An agency's job is to create tension between internal stakeholders and external team members while keeping all parties focused on the same, single-minded goal. This often necessitates challenging assumptions, questioning process efficiency, and asking uncomfortable questions—all in pursuit of a product or campaign worthy of influencing decision-makers and impacting genuine, meaningful change.

Several different advertising agencies will support your go-to-market plans. A full-service advertising agency is a "jack of all trades," specializing in every aspect of online and offline marketing and advertising. These agencies are typically on retainer and piece together teams designed to support large-scale projects, whether creating a new website, a portal for customer service, an event, or an advertising campaign.

If your business needs some kind of everything, then choosing an ad agency that offers a range of services is the best way to go, but you will not be a hero if you take for granted that your bloated "agency" of record will piece together the team you need when you need it. It is essential to be an educated consumer and work the system as much as you need to. I worked with the expensive and vetted agency of record on prominent products like multi-year website builds, strategies, and campaigns across multiple regions and markets. I worked with an internal production agency that was very good at taking the big ideas and concepts of the expensive global agency and creating programs from them. And then, there was a stable of specialized partners in the system. Whether working with internally provided agency services or taking advantage of economies of scale, the choice is yours.

Remember, however, that even though you may be able to "save" by working with your lower-cost partners, it is also on you to deliver the project seamlessly. If you choose to divert agency resources and things don't go well, you will be associated with the project. So, in the beginning, it would make sense for you to establish your criteria for how you work. Also, remember that there are special agencies you should consider hiring when your larger agency is not specialized enough.

Please note that there is a difference between doing business with a regular freelancer and a company that is ready, willing, and able to work with corporations. To work with a corporation, the company needs to have been vetted, signed many agreements, and given assurances that they are doing business in a way that is aligned with the company's best interest. The idea of having the right insurance for a company might be the difference between hiring someone and not hiring someone. It is not as simple as creating marketing at a corporation. In many ways, it is less about how and what you say and more about creativity and how you get things done because of all the restrictions, rules, regulations, and ethical practices you must do to be associated with this company.

Working with a big agency is only sometimes the best way to get what you need done. Although they may have many services available, it is essential to look beyond what they can offer and make sure that partnering with them will bring enough expertise. When it comes to social media, using multiple separate providers that specialize specifically in one thing can often bring better results than trusting an all-encompassing agency when it comes to providing top-quality products and services. Doing so ensures that each provider is experienced in their area and able to provide the best possible solution for the particular need.

Here are a few examples of technical talent that you could find in the marketplace.

Blogging/content creation

Blogging services allow individuals to create blogs to share information about themselves and their interests. Companies also hire writers to write blog posts for them. These posts can include news updates, company announcements, and more.

Email newsletters

An email newsletter service allows users to send newsletters to customers. Users can choose how frequently they receive newsletters and what content they receive.

Podcasting

A podcasting service allows users to upload audio files to the internet so that others can listen to them. Podcasts are similar to radio shows, except that listeners can access podcasts whenever they want instead of listening live.

SEO/SEM

When it comes to the world of digital marketing, no one should underestimate the importance of SEO (search engine optimization) and SEM (search engine marketing). Whether you are a budding marketer or an experienced advertising executive, these two elements offer immense potential when it comes to increasing brand visibility and awareness. In order to make the most out of these tools, though, companies need to have a person or a team who understands how they work and knows how to keep up with algorithm changes, as well as new trends such as artificial intelligence (AI). This person or team needs to be able to stay abreast of new technologies that can affect how customers find and consume information online.

SEO is a key part of any digital marketing strategy, as it helps businesses get their website ranking higher in relevant search engine results. It does this by creating websites with content that contains keywords that customers are likely searching for. SEO also studies customer behavior, so that brands can better understand what kind of content they should produce if they want their website showing up at the top of relevant searches.

SEM takes things further by helping brands create effective campaigns using search engine advertising tools such as Google Ads and Bing Ads. This form of advertising allows businesses to speak with and address specific audiences according to search queries and other interests/demographics. The ads show up on results pages whenever users enter certain keywords in their search queries—giving them more visibility than non-advertised results.

These techniques not only help with increased visibility but also with analyzing customer behavior and preferences—crucial components for businesses that want to get ahead in today's competitive digital landscape.

Example: AI/bots

An AI agency can help a brand project by using artificial intelligence and machine learning to inform decision-making. This can create better customer experiences, identify potential opportunities, facilitate product development and marketing, automate processes, increase efficiency, and more. AI agencies specialize in researching topics related to brand objectives which they use to make data-driven predictions and improvements. They might also employ natural language processing to conduct sentiment analysis on social media posts related to the brand.

A corporate team knows the ins and outs of what works and what doesn't in the corporation's walls and is responsible for bringing ideas to life in the organization's reality. What typically happens for a project is that a digital team will be tasked with finding the right agency in partnership with sourcing or procurement. Then they will hire and brief the agency to bring the products to life. In a typical agency, there are many roles. Listed below is not all-inclusive but will give you a good idea of who to look for and what to expect from your agency team on a branding project.

Account director

The account director role is one of the important positions in advertising agencies. This person manages the client relationship and ensures that the creative work meets the client's needs. They also manage the budget and ensure that it is spent wisely. In addition to managing the client relationship, the account director must also oversee the production process. They ensure that the creative work is delivered on time and within budget. They also help develop the creative strategy and ensure it aligns with the brand objectives. The account director must also understand how technology works and the tools to produce effective campaigns. For example, some clients prefer to hire an external vendor to handle their digital marketing rather than having an internal team do it. In short, the account director is the glue that holds everything together. They work closely with the creative teams, production departments, technology specialists, marketers, salespeople, and everyone involved in creating ads. Some focus solely on digital media; others specialize in print campaigns. Still others manage both traditional and online marketing.

Strategists

An agency strategist develops and implements marketing plans to promote clients' brands through campaigns, product launches, or other initiatives. They research the ideal audiences, analyze data related to the project goals, create a brand story, suggest strategies and tactics to meet those goals, work with the creative teams to implement their ideas, and recommend changes and improvements in their project execution based on market feedback. In addition, they often act as a liaison between the client and campaign staff.

Production

One of the roles of an agency project manager is to be responsible for every aspect of the branding rollout. This includes managing budgets and timelines, keeping stakeholders updated on progress, and interfacing with vendors such as printing houses and media outlets. Additionally, you must ensure that everything meets clients' goals and deadlines, as well as quality standards and the agreed-upon design specifications while still having creative flair that makes the branding stand out.

Technologists

The role of an agency technologist in a branding project involves providing technical solutions, strategizing, developing digital marketing campaigns, and analyzing the results. They should be able to stay ahead of trends and technologies while offering insight into ways to create a successful brand identity. Agency technologists must also ensure that all marketing efforts comply with regulatory standards and industry guidelines. In addition, they spearhead new technology projects related to website development or software tools for client acquisition.

Creative directors

The creative director plays an important role: they are responsible for shaping the overall feel and look of the brand. The creative director will oversee the entire team, lead brainstorming sessions, and help define a unified message reflecting the project's goals. They will develop the visual assets and identify key channels to attract potential customers. Additionally, they will be responsible for monitoring trends to create a successful brand strategy.

Copywriters

Copywriters serve a unique role in branding projects, as they are responsible for refining and bringing the brand's message to life with words. They use their strong writing skills to ensure that copy is clear, punchy, and conveys the brand's value. When molding a brand's messaging, a copywriter carefully considers elements such as tone of voice, style guides, and even audience inclination. They work closely with designers to add language to visuals and ensure design assets stay on-brand. With both creative and technical abilities, a talented copywriter plays an integral part in bringing a compelling brand story to life.

Measurement

The measurement team is responsible for tracking and analyzing brand KPIs to monitor and improve the success of the branding effort. The team will regularly analyze different types of data, such as customer feedback, website analytics, sales records, etc., to assess the effectiveness of brand campaigns and refine tactics accordingly. Additionally, they play an essential role in helping senior management quantify returns on investment from different branding initiatives.

Your agency may be a part of a holding company. In many situations, the holding company will attempt to support every project you will work on. An agency holding company is an organization that owns multiple advertising agencies. Each independent company provides a range of development, project management, storytelling, and presenting services to clients, such as creating campaigns, running digital and traditional media campaigns, helping with branding, marketing research, and more. A holding company can offer its clients access to resources from each company. This helps them serve their clients better and provide a better product at a lower cost.

But there's a possibility that the whole "economies of scale" promised by the holding company may never be seen. Many agencies are making sure they don't lose their retainer, which has much waste built in and typically doesn't account for incentives to do their best work in the quickest amount of time. In my experience, most agencies never say they can't take on the job. An agency doesn't have the DNA to reflect on the client's needs and where they need to be. The easiest thing for an agency to do is to go to their stable of freelancers and assign the work to one of them at a premium rate. Most freelancers work the circuit of agencies, and many are very talented, but their talent is only as good as how they are briefed and how their success is evaluated.

So, if you ask your agency to develop an app for you, you are not buying a successful app and all the infrastructure and staff required to stand up the app, serve customers, update it for new technology, have a steady drumbeat of content, etc. Instead, you will likely spend hundreds of thousands of dollars on clickable prototypes. If you are working with one of the top-tier agencies and your hands are tied, try the process out, and see where you end up, but be aware that ultimately, you are accountable for delivering results, not clickable prototypes. Eventually, you will need to condition your stakeholders to agree that building an app is a multi-year endeavor requiring fundamental changes to the business to support it. The trick is to let the top-tier agency create the prototype and then work with a hungry agency with a tried-and-true specialty in creating apps to bring the product to life.

Another big agency trick is establishing special teams that bring together many people from different agencies within the holding company. This is all good until some money is up for grabs, and the participating agencies fight for the money to meet their goals. I have noticed agency inciting in situations designed to make it easier for the client. The only way that we're going to make something like this work is to create incentives as a team and be able to stick to them.

Meaning establishing goals and financial incentives together as a team and bonuses that can be attained when results are achieved.

When selecting partners, you must ensure they are assimilated within your company. Using an Excel spreadsheet as deliverables is not helpful, and you should hold your partners accountable for using your systems. When you write your request for proposal (RFP), it is essential to set requirements that commit them to use this tech stack. Great content is only as good as its ability to be measured.

It is not enough to design a great system; having the right leadership to consider all the factors by which customers interact is critical. This also goes to what I said earlier about multi-year projects and obtaining the support to deliver the project. The special sauce is having people with broad experiences who can navigate each specialty to drive integration and interactivity.

Before you engage any stakeholders, it is up to you to set the tone and establish a hypothesis for what problem we are solving, why we are solving it, and why they need to join you on this journey. It would be best if you remembered that people inherently don't understand branding, so it will be up to you to use some of the same storytelling techniques you've learned in this book to figure out how to build strong relationships with key stakeholders from within and outside your company.

You should also know that many agencies worldwide specialize in branding. If your company can afford it, I recommend you try it, but if you can't do all the things we're talking about here with your buy-in, a loyal team, and strong agency support, you will be able to accomplish what you need to.

But if you decide to hire an agency, don't look at this as something you can "outsource." You must fully participate in the process, roll up your sleeves, and deeply understand everything your agency will do on your behalf. You could be missing out on a valuable foundation of knowledge that will take you very far as an employee. There is something about finding information and connecting dots for yourself that will never be accomplished if you simply ask someone else to do the work.

There is a statement of work template on page XXX. Whether you go with an agency or establish an internal team, this document will be critical to level-set expectations and role clarity.

Budget

The cost of a branding effort can vary greatly, depending on your specific needs and creative strategy. Professional branding efforts can be anything from a few thousand to tens of millions of dollars, depending on the project's scope, size, and length. Professional branding often includes research studies or surveys, extensive brand development processes, and tactics such as logo design, website design, and copywriting services.

Thinking globally

When creating a global brand, it is essential to have international representation in a branding project because it allows for more diverse insight and perspectives when creating an effective global brand. When done right, branding will have a long-lasting and positive impact on the company's image. Representation from different countries can ensure that diverse views are considered when constructing a powerful brand identity. It also increases the chance of broad customer acceptance and engagement with the message/visuals presented by the brand.

Some thoughts on timing

Having a comprehensive and realistic timeline for any branding effort is essential. Generally, creating a brand identity can take anywhere from three to six months, depending on the project's scope. This includes discovering who you are as a business and what you want your brand to stand for, researching to inform branding decisions, designing visual assets, and more. The most important takeaway is that any brand identity effort should thoroughly create an effective result.

Some thoughts on the scope

Securing a reliable partner to complete your agency RFP (request for proposal) is an essential decision for any business. Before finding a suitable agency, ask yourself the right questions. Defining a clear set of criteria and objectives specific to your goals will make narrowing down potential candidates easier. Once you have this information ready, start connecting with possible contenders—utilize recommendations from peers, scan through relevant portfolios and articulate your vision through a series of interviews. After the initial selection round, invite the most promising companies to present their take on your RFP. Quality communication and a thorough assessment will help ensure you make the right choice in an agency partner.

Building your team

After the proposal is drafted, the next step is to have a kick-off meeting with key organizational stakeholders. But the question is, whom should you invite, and what should you expect from the stakeholders?

When deciding how many people should be on a branding committee, it is essential to consider the team size. A smaller team of only three or four members may be ideal for smaller projects, while a larger team of six or more people could work well for larger, more complex ones.

The branding project's type and focus should also be considered when determining how many people should be on the team. For example, if the branding project is focused mainly on creating a website, it might make sense to have user experience designers or web developers as part of the team.

TABLE 8.1

Background	Company leverages its strong market position to develop a professional community, enhance its executive reputation, and establish an authoritative industry presence to drive the narrative on important industry topics, trends, and future outlooks.
	This initiative will focus on establishing a brand identity while supporting efforts to extend its core capabilities and provide foundations for future growth opportunities.
Initiative Goals	• Establishment of a storytelling brand construct • Consistent content development and publication • Creation of value for diverse audiences
	Develop a strategy and programming roadmap yielding an ownable industry voice, narrative, and POV on various relevant topics. Your Brand Coach's consulting remit will follow a phased approach:
The Assignment	**Phase 1: Discovery and Assessment** • Internal audit of past and present corporate comms activity • Industry landscape overview + competitive analysis (companies + industry execs) • White space: what is the sweet spot for the company? **Phase 2: Strategy Development** • WHAT (are we going to say): creating story arches + narrative • HOW are we going to tell it: establishing our voice(s) • WHEN + WHERE are we going to show up: action plan including recommended topics, content calendar, and development resources • Define KPIs and success metrics

Discovery workshop(s)

Session designed to solicit input, ensuring that company's strategy aligns with the enterprise roadmap.

- Working session(s) with key stakeholders
- Outline the company's communication and social media goals
- Examine existing and planned company business activities
- Discuss thought leadership philosophy and vision for branding
- Define the aspirational role of key digital and communication channels

Deliverable: Read-out document identifying key learnings and creating alignment for the remainder of the planning process.

Market intelligence

- Internal audit: analyze past/present/planned activity across relevant corporate communications channels and executive leadership team profiles
- Platform assessment: best-in-class ecosystems, trends, innovations
- Global insurance category: analyze our competition
- Audience analysis: who are our internal stakeholders + external community and what do they care about?
- Identify white space

Deliverable: Custom market intelligence report

Phase 1 estimated timing: 4 weeks

Storytelling approach—company

Leveraging established white space, developing a story narrative to build a thought leadership platform, and generating engagement.

- Positioning: foundational narrative
- Apply and build upon story arc, key themes, and messages for the ideal audience(s)
- Voice: leveraging brand guidelines + executive personas

Phase 1: Discovery and Assessment

(continued)

TABLE 8.1 (Continued)

	Strategic framework
	Putting the puzzle together
	
	• Key messaging map: narrative, voice, content themes, timelines
	• Editorial calendar including quarterly and monthly themes
	• Community building and engagement tactics
	• Channels
	   ○ PR
	   ○ social channels
	   ○ white papers
	   ○ speeches
	   ○ paid media support considerations
	• KPI framework to track global performance and impact
	• Resource requirements for building content assets, publishing, and community management

Phase 2: Strategy Development	**Campaign kick-off** • Asset creation • Editorial calendar • Community management and posting of content • Work with executives to extend the content ideas presented Deliverable: Comprehensive action plan with messaging themes, calendars, budget, and resource recommendations as well as the implementation. **Phase 2 estimated timing: 8 weeks**

Proposed Terms

Timing

Your Brand Coach team:

- Content + brand building
- Market intelligence + planning + project management

Lastly, it's wise to think about having people from different departments and areas, such as marketing, IT, and design represented; including different perspectives can help ensure that no stone is left unturned in forming an effective brand strategy.

- What is done in-house? Based on the descriptors above, who and how many key stakeholders do you want and need on your team to get the job done?

- What does an agency do? Based on the many types of agencies out there and their different roles, will you pick a specialized agency? A more general agency? Be realistic about what you ask for and how much money you have.

- What does a production firm do? An outsourced production firm can be a great option when cost-prohibitive agencies are not feasible. A creative director can come up with the concept, brand architecture, and other higher-level tasks that require more expertise, then assign tasks to an external team—such as copywriting or design work—for implementation. This division of labor can save time and money while allowing for the ideas to still be executed appropriately.

Remember that only some people need to be on the committee. A good rule of thumb when selecting who is on your committee is to consider whether you want their opinion and need their strategic guidance or whether you need some stakeholders to get it done for you when you need it. You can engage those stakeholders when you need them or ask your key stakeholders on the committee to find and engage a specialist.

If you are the marketing leader, it is your job to create this agenda. Suppose you are the marketing leader that hires the agency; in that case, you are ultimately accountable for what is on the agenda and what comes from the meeting, so you must spend the time upfront to ensure that the agenda is taking your cause further. For example, here is a high-level agenda you can use to build your own.

- Intro—a team slide with our short bios
- Approach to building strategies

- ○ Discovery + assessment leading to white space definition
- ○ Framework: building blocks aligning business + marketing + audience + channels
- ○ Go to market
- Market intelligence (see chapter 9 on research)
  - ○ Macro overview of LinkedIn usage in corporate America (or global?)—sizing + trends
  - ○ Best in class (industry agnostic)
  - ○ Competitive analysis
  - ○ Ideal audience
  - ○ Company comm ecosystem
- White space
  - ○ Where can we compete and win?
  - ○ What are the key insights that substantiate our position?
  - ○ How do we align the business?
  - ○ How does a brand carve out a relevant niche?
  - ○ Leading to "What is our story"?
- Your industry—current conditions
- Overview of the company and business lines/ How does the company make money?
- Competition
- Marketing
  - ○ Current plans—campaigns, social media, thought leadership
  - ○ Past successes
  - ○ Looking ahead
- Audience
  - ○ Customers
  - ○ Strategic partners
- What else should we know about?
- Next steps

Charter time

To kick off the process, you should create a charter. The charter is who is working on the project, when, and how. There is no right or wrong way to do it. However, it is essential to have a senior leader who can and will go to bat for the project when needed and has a line of sight and authority to make budget decisions. It would be best if you also considered that people move roles and jobs in most companies. If this happens, say congratulations to the person who left, and then look at the roles in the charter and find someone who can step in and take the project forward. This is especially important if you expect your project to roll out and evolve for many years, and most projects like this are not short term.

Identify the following in the charter:

- group norms
- the project timeline and roadmap
- who is on the team
- what their roles and responsibilities are
- the deadline
- the scope of the project
- the situation today

At a minimum, a project charter should define scope, budget, schedule, and technical aspects. The best project charters are short and to the point, often outlining or using bulleted lists of the planned major design or technical features. The finished project charter should contain the goals statement from the planning phase, as well as the structural details of the site.

As the leader of this project, you need to take the initiative to start the charter and then give the committee you form an opportunity to react to what you share, provide their voice, and put their mark on it.

Knowing your audience's habits and preferences is critical to designing a successful brand. Taking an analytical approach by evaluating market research data helps inform creative storytelling techniques that will help attract customers and keep them happy. So here we are. You understand where you are and where you fit in the organization; you have an agency to support you; you have a committee to manage the brand; now it's time to dig deeper and make an actionable plan. This plan involves researching consumer insights and trends, considering social media data, and also customer feedback. With research in place, you can create content that resonates with your audience and engages them emotionally. This starts and ends with market research!

09

Research and Measurement

So here we are. You understand where you are and where you fit in the organization; you have an agency to support you; you have a committee to manage the brand; now it's time to dig deeper and make an actionable plan. This plan involves researching consumer insights and trends, considering social media data and customer feedback. With research in place, we can create content that resonates with your audience and engages them emotionally.

Market research plays a critical role in every business's success, enabling companies to plan strategically for the future and adjust their strategy when needed based on consumer feedback. Research allows organizations to better understand consumer needs, preferences, and trends. It enables them to create marketing campaigns and innovative products or services that will help them meet those needs. Using data gathered from market research studies, companies can better target and tailor their messaging, discover what marketing strategies work best, and gain a competitive edge. Market research also helps identify unmet needs and offers insights into how they can be addressed through new products, services, or pricing or distribution channel changes.

You can unlock the power of intelligence with data-driven decision-making with market research. It can provide insights into competitor behavior and trends, customer needs and behaviors, market attractiveness, industry size, or brand preferences. Some fundamental best practices and principles should be considered to create an optimal market research setting that will yield truly valuable insights. This includes crafting a clear research plan with stated objectives and methodologies agreed upon by everyone involved; selecting reliable sampling techniques; eliminating potential biases; properly constructing questionnaires; selecting relevant parameters for analysis; utilizing empirical data wherever possible; framing questions appropriately; and accounting for weather and other considerations.

While it is critical to understand business fundamentals like comprehending the business and its goal, analysis of the market, competitors, and customers, an operational plan outlining tactics to be deployed, and financial projections and budgeting, make sure to focus more of your energy on brand and marketing research. This involves understanding the ideas expressed, who your audience is, the mode of communication, what colors are selected, the sentimentality conveyed, and the style employed.

To truly engage with your audience and ensure they understand your observations thoroughly, it is essential to explain each picture or example you include; by connecting the visuals directly with their associated points of discussion, the elements of your research support one another for a cohesive narrative experience. Additionally, discussing specific details such as color variation or shape can further demonstrate how what is displayed is connected to a larger framework. Moreover, pointing out any discrepancies observed within these elements further improves understanding for those who may need to be made aware of what these differences may mean beyond their literal meaning when taken at face value.

It is essential to build research into your daily life. Be curious and think about what technology people use today and how those technologies have shifted. For example, as a father, I watch my children play different types of games than I played when I was a kid. When I was a kid, the games were *Super Mario Brothers* or Mike Tyson's *Punch Out*, which were straightforward games with established levels and a hierarchy of what you can and can't do. My children today play games like *Roblox* and *Minecraft*. These games have a different outcome because they allow anyone who plays them to create whatever their mind wants to make. In addition to playing them, these games are typically open source and allow people with creativity to build worlds and constructs for others to play in. I'm wonderstruck by our world today, which allows for a lot more creativity and fluidity than the world I grew up in as a child. So, when you think about what customers want to do and how customers change behavior, and you have a company designed for a paradigm where people played *Super Mario Brothers*, it should force you to think about how people want to play the game today.

Think like an anthropologist

Diversity of thought and perspective is critical here; to get unexpected insights or even to understand details of your business that a typical employee wouldn't see, it is essential to think like an anthropologist. Anthropology is the study of what makes us human, including culture, language, behavior, and social interactions, to name a few. Taking an anthropological approach would mean understanding people through their preferences about what constructs their worldviews and opinions. This is a foil to dishonest marketing, where the business projects and imposes its understanding of what the customer needs instead of discovering what drives them. Here you will need to understand culture, beliefs, rituals, and shared outlooks that can be observed and described. How can you find these anthropological gems? As an anthropological thinker, you must ensure you can view things objectively and understand multiple perspectives on specific topics. It's essential to consider diversity of thought when exploring a given culture or environment to gain new insights into how people interact with one another and understand the world around them.

- What do people think?
- What do people feel?
- What do people do?
- When do they do it?
- Why do they do it?

What do people think?

Anthropological thinking involves considering how different groups of people think differently. This means understanding what an individual might think or feel and what characters, minorities, and majorities are thinking about. Critical analysis of different viewpoints is necessary to understand all angles before concluding.

What do people feel?

The emotions that people feel can also provide insight into why certain behaviors occur and what motivates individuals to act in the ways they do. In some cases, emotions play a crucial role in creating changing social networks that allow for new ideologies to be expressed. Interpreting the feelings behind behavior bridges understanding and disagreement, providing more appreciation and respect for all cultures worldwide, even when they conflict with each other's views.

What do people do?

In addition to understanding thoughts and feelings, it's essential to consider actions taken to gain a clearer picture of how humans interact with their environment. How can specific trends or issues be explained through activities? Exploring these behaviors provides insight into how vital information is spread through society, influencing communication patterns between members within communities and cultures across countries or continents.[1]

When do they do it?

Time is arguably just as important as any other factor when understanding anthropological thinking—especially when determining why things happen at certain times instead of others or how specific timeframes create separation between generations within a culture or environment. Thinking critically about this aspect typically sheds light on broader trends regarding change within societies over time and investigations into current events that signal potential shifts due to generational differences or legacies left behind through history books or traditional belief systems which still have significant impact today, even after centuries gone by.

Why do they do it?

Finally, the question comes back full circle—why? People do what they do for various reasons, including being motivated by money, power, pleasure, or knowledge. People may also be driven by emotional needs such as security, love, and acceptance. Ultimately, everyone's decisions are based on their values and beliefs.

Going deeper

Your brand's purpose is to establish an emotional connection with your audience by creating and delivering a clear, consistent message that resonates with them and meets their needs. Your brand should represent the values and ethics behind your business, differentiate you from the competition, and amplify your voice in the marketplace.

A clear research plan with stated objectives and methodologies agreed upon by everyone involved

Understanding the challenge you are attempting to solve is essential before your research can be completed, and gaining clarity is a significant part of that. Transparency will help improve your understanding of yourself and let your audience understand you better. Creating an effective market research brief with clear action steps is critical for any successful market research project.

My market research process is as follows.

- Identify an issue, discuss alternatives, and set out research objectives
- Develop a research program

- Gather information
- Choose appropriate market research techniques
- Organize and analyze information and data
- Present findings
- Decide based on the research
- Do it

Identify an issue

What is the difference between good market research and bad? A good question (get it?). The best market research answers a specific question with significance to your organization. When the scope of a market research project is narrow enough, the insights gained may need to be more general to be useful. When looking for insights from market research, it's essential to narrow the scope and focus on specific areas or topics that can provide meaningful results. A narrowly defined market research effort is likely to yield more detailed, actionable insights than one that is too broad.

The first step is to identify the problem. This can be done by asking yourself questions such as:

- What are we trying to achieve?
- How will we know when it has been achieved?
- Who is responsible for achieving this goal?
- What resources do we need to accomplish this goal?
- What are your organization's mission and values?
- How will this project support your mission?
- What are the two or three most important goals for the project?
- Who is the primary audience?
- What do you want the audience to think or do after being exposed to your brand?

When you look at the list, it should become evident to you (even an outsider who has done very little research on the company) that the problem the company has depends on the age of the company, the industry, how established it is, etc.

Are you looking to increase recognition or reputation, address a crisis, refresh your brand, improve customer experience, or introduce new products or services? If you answered yes to any of these, then this guide is just what you need.

- Increase recognition or reputation: The first step in increasing recognition or reputation is to create an effective marketing campaign. This includes campaigns that are both creative and engaging. Additionally, the campaign should focus on the messages and values of your brand that people can connect with emotionally. Ultimately, customers should be able to recognize and relate to your company quickly through seeing, hearing, and feeling it in their daily lives.

- Address a crisis: If an issue in your company could damage its reputation among customers (e.g. layoffs), it's important to be transparent about what's going on while also using positive language when possible—don't make claims without evidence! Additionally, carefully curate any newsworthy events related to the crisis so that only proper information gets out there from reliable sources. Consider setting up a separate contact page for follow-up inquiries about the incident with further information.

- Refresh your brand: Start by doing an audit of your current branding—review visuals such as logos and color palettes, messaging such as slogans, and communications pieces such as website posts, then decide if any tweaks need to be made for more modernity or relevancy with today's audiences.

- Improve customer experience: When it comes to improving customer experience, make sure you identify what specific needs must be fulfilled by providing helpful support options (forums/chatbots), customized self-service materials (FAQs), simplified checkout processes etc. You'll also want to introduce innovative technologies like AI-powered search engines where applicable—so inquirers get prompt responses no matter how complex their queries may be.

Introduce new products or services: Whether introducing entirely new or leveraging existing products/services, think about how providing something differentiated can help gain market share. Find out what competitors offer and evaluate ways yours might be enhanced significantly. Do additional research into rapidly changing industry standards and regulations and consult professionals capable of accurately forecasting technological developments etc. to develop differentiated product/service offerings.

Measuring the success of marketing campaigns can be difficult, but it is essential to understand how your strategies are performing. To accurately measure success, focus on setting specific objectives such as increasing customer engagement and building brand awareness. By setting challenging but achievable goals, you will be able to assess the results of your campaign and use this data to inform future decisions.

A deeper look into why and how

Have you ever wondered why or how specific problems or situations happen? While it is essential to identify potential solutions, it's also beneficial to try and analyze the cause of the problem. Getting to the root of a problem can be time-consuming but will help individuals and organizations in the long term.

When looking for solutions to any problem, it is essential not to forget about analyzing what caused them in the first place. Understanding each circumstance and determining how it happened can be critical when finding strategies for prevention in future cases.

INTERNAL CHANGES

Research is often spurred by changes within the company. It could be that you've replaced product components or changed your manufacturing process, leading to a need to make sure your customers are still satisfied with the result. Studies can also help see how new strategies could increase revenue and customer satisfaction.

EXTERNAL FORCES

Necessary research also comes from external forces such as economic downturns and changes in market trends. It may become necessary to investigate customer buying histories or preferences, as well as changing financial situations if people can no longer pay for your products or services.

TECHNOLOGY ADVANCEMENTS

One of the driving forces behind research needs is technological advancements and their rapid evolution over time. Companies must stay ahead of the curve when it comes to staying relevant and offering the best products or services on the market. This can involve recognizing shifts in consumer behaviors and purchasing decisions due to technological changes.

SOCIETAL NORMS

Research into societal norms is necessary as they shift or change over time, influencing customer behavior and even ethics standards among companies and their competitors. Researching emerging trends can help you better understand how different generations perceive value differently, which helps create a more comprehensive marketing strategy for appealing to everyone involved with your product or service offerings.

GLOBAL EVENTS

Global events have an enormous effect on influencing consumer tastes, including public health crises such as pandemics that limit consumer spending habits temporarily but also reshape them in ways that will affect consumer choices in the future in specific categories permanently. If something affects global mobility, this will shape how companies approach their research tasks too, so staying abreast of current events is key in ensuring all needed information is collected accurately and quickly when required by market research and insights teams.

CUSTOMER RECOGNITION AND LOYALTY

An essential component of research involves exploring how well-known your company's brand is among potential customers, how many recognize it when given a cue versus those who had never heard it before, as well as whether existing consumers remain loyal or if they opt for another provider instead at any point during their journey with you. Completing surveys on brand recognition through social media channels such as Facebook Messenger can provide helpful insights into the effectiveness of your marketing campaigns.

MONEY

It's essential to understand what kind of spending existing clients are putting towards marketing and branding and what realistic price points work for attracting new buyers. Analyzing past sales turnover numbers, analyzing seasonality data, conducting contextual customer interviews, and A/B testing practices all come together to help leaders understand where their growth rate stands comparatively to both internal goals and external competition.

So, what is your research problem?

Jeremiah Genest's article "Problem Statement Framing"[2] discusses the importance of framing problems that businesses face so that their solutions can be identified efficiently and effectively. Genest explains the value of applying a problem-oriented discussion to uncover unknown elements, the benefit of conducting detailed background research, and an iterative process for going from a vague initial statement to a structured one. He further promotes taking time to re-examine assumptions and not just jump into solutions. Genest's article explains how to properly frame problem statements to maximize the chance for success in solving any situation.

Try to fill out the table below and then when you are done make your problem sentence into one sentence.

TABLE 9.1

	Typical questions	Contains
Who?	Who are the people directly concerned with the problem? Who does this? Who should be involved but wasn't? Was someone involved who shouldn't be?	Roles and departments
What?	What happened?	Action, steps, description
When?	When did the problem occur?	Times, dates, places In process (e.g. happening now)
Where?	Where did the problem occur?	Location
Why is it important?	Why did we do this? What are the requirements? What is the expected condition?	Justification, reason
How?	How did we discover it? Where in the process was it?	Method, process, procedure
How many? How much?	How many things are involved? How often did the situation happen? How much did it impact?	Number, frequency

Unlock insight by documenting your research plan

Gathering reliable data is one of the most critical steps for successful decision-making. A clear plan will ensure that everything required for effective decision-making is collected.

Define your goals and objectives

Outline this project's goals and objectives so they are crystal clear. Setting realistic goals is essential so they can be easily tracked throughout the process. Once goals have been established, it's time to decide what objectives will best help achieve them, such as research, development of marketing materials, or customer surveys. Additionally, ensure you develop a timeline for completing each goal's associated objective so that progress can be monitored easily over time.

Determine scope and detail tasks

Now it's time to get into more detail by determining exactly what needs to be done to complete each task associated with strengthening and supporting your overall branding efforts on an ongoing basis. Make sure deadlines are added so everyone involved knows when key deliverables should be completed to keep things moving forward at a steady pace across all stakeholders involved in your project's success as we advance!

Estimate timeline and budget

Time and budget are key components to any successful research project. Knowing how to create an effective timeline and budget while identifying who will perform the research and what methods they will use are instructions that can help bring your project to life. Start by estimating the time you need for the project and its associated costs. There are a variety of different factors that you'll need to consider when estimating your timeline and budget, including the complexity of the task; the number of people participating in the project; availability of resources; training needed; schedule constraints (e.g. do you have deadlines that have to be met); data collection methods used; potential travel involved; technology needs, etc.

Identify who will perform the research

After you've calculated an estimate for your timeline and budget, it's essential to determine who will lead or participate in the research process… not just staff members or team members, but also outside consultants or individuals if needed. Consider factors like skill set/ experience level (or lack thereof), knowledge of a specific industry or topic area, motivation level, etc. when making this decision. Please also see chapter 8 on agency support for guidelines on how to select an agency.

Your marketing intelligence outline and recommendations

Having a well-crafted marketing plan is essential for any successful branding project. But having an effective market research and intelligence plan is just as essential to ensure that your execution rounds out the planning process towards success.

Having an effective market research and intelligence plan will give you invaluable insights into potential customers, competitive landscapes, and overall strategies to develop sustainable marketing models that work. Here is a closer look at how to devise an effective market research and intelligence plan.

To devise the best plan to achieve your goals, consider the resources you can use with Jon Yanovsky's approach.[3] I just decided to brand it the Yanovsky Method. By understanding your ideal market and potential customers, you can determine which strategies are necessary

TABLE 9.2

Slide #	Key message	Content
1	Frame assignment	50K-foot view Executive summary
2	How did we get here?	Why are we doing this... the background • What do you sell? Think emotionally not factually • Describe the product in detail: ◦ Who is it for? ◦ What are the company's offerings other than the product of focus? ◦ How much does it cost? ◦ Where can you buy it? ◦ What do customers think about the company? Look at its ratings • What are the company values? • What is the business model? • What is the corporate history? • Who is in charge? • What is the vision? • What is the point of differentiation of the company?

(continued)

TABLE 9.2 (Continued)

Slide #	Key message	Content
3	Assignment	What are we doing? How does this product market itself and establish a brand?What's the problem? • Why is research needed? • What problem needs to be solved? • How will we know if the problem is solved?
		NEW SECTION: Trends and insights
4	Trends we should consider	3—5 macro trends/strategies • What's their slogan? • What colors do they use? • Who are the most prominent executives? What are they saying about the brand? • Who else is talking about the brand and what are they saying? • Show some examples of top-performing social media • Show some examples of top-performing content. What made it perform well? • Show some examples of poorly performing content. Why do you think it performed poorly? • How is your brand connected with what's going on today in society? • How is your brand ready for the future?
5—8	Trend slides	1. Qual: Overview of trend 2. Quant: 2+ key macro stats (sizing the trend) 3. Big visuals
		NEW SECTION: Best in class
9	Overview	What does it look like to be best in class to address the assignment? What tactics do they use? • Show an example of an ad • Show an example of content created • Pull available stats on how they perform
10—13	Case studies	One mini case study per bucket of best-in-class criteria.
14	Best practices	Summary of case study company efforts that we can apply to the brand and problem we are solving (will be a "white space building block")

(continued)

TABLE 9.2 (Continued)

Slide #	Key message	Content
		NEW SECTION: Competitive landscape
15	Set up slide	List of competitors we will be exploring
16	Competitive analysis	Chart of all competitors on 1—2 slides Key competitors—business details • Who? • Where do they do business? • Who are their customers? • What business results do they have? • What is their strategy in a sentence or two? • How are they better than your brand? • How are they worse? • What is different about them?
17	What we learned	Key learnings from the competitive analysis (will be a "white space building block") For each competitor, list their brand footprint in less detail than your brand but enough to learn where and how you promote your product: • Product • Price • Place • Promotion • Creative strategy • Market of focus • Benefits • Support • Tone
		NEW SECTION: Audience
18	Persona chart	Type of content produced, content consumed, narrative style, etc. Consideration: profile a couple of real-life examples of persona Who is the audience? • Who are we talking to? • Who is your ideal customer? • Consider age, gender, income, etc., as well as psychographic information such as lifestyle preferences and interests • What are their motivations, goals, and challenges?

(continued)

TABLE 9.2 (Continued)

Slide #	Key message	Content
19	What we learned	Key learnings from audience analysis (will be a "white space building block")
		NEW SECTION: White space
20	What we know	Topline summary of macro takeaways from the report
21	Building blocks	Trends, best practices, competitive, audience
22	White space	Triangulating our findings + hypothesis
23	Creative/strategy	How are we going to show up: what do we stand for, tone, narrative, storytelling?
24-26	Territory exploration	2—3 themes/threads (bringing the consideration filters from the previous slide to life)
27	Where do we go from here?	What needs to happen next?

to create a strong brand presence. Remember that no matter how thorough your planning is, taking active steps is necessary to make any branding project successful.

Choose appropriate market research techniques

When determining the best marketing research techniques for a brand project, it is important to consider your objectives, budget, and audience. A good starting point would be to conduct market research through surveys and focus groups on ascertaining consumer preferences. This will allow you to gain insights into consumer needs and desires, helping you to design your brand project effectively. Consider conducting secondary research by examining industry profiles and trends to gain additional information about competitors and current market conditions. Finally, consider using social media analytics tools such as Facebook Insights or Twitter Analytics to obtain further data regarding consumer behavior online. There are many ways to perform market research.[4] Companies can determine who their customers are and how they think through these processes. Qualitative analysis looks at non-numerical data from sources such as interviews, open-ended surveys, etc. to understand qualitative interpretation patterns regarding topics studied, thereby providing us with more subtle insight/experience into people's behaviors than quantitative approaches do alone.

Secondary research is a good place to start for basic demographics and details about your industry, like market size and significant players, so you can understand where you fit in and, on a high level, how to differentiate yourself in the space.

- What are the top three topics being discussed repeatedly in your industry?
- What are the three most significant problems in your industry?
- Who are the three most prominent players in your industry?

With this, you can learn age, gender, highest level of education, employment status, annual household income/annual business income, relationship status, whether they have children, etc. Do they rent or own? What type of community do they live in? Are they planning on investing in your type of product or service shortly? Which social media platforms do they use? How active are they online?

Primary research could be collecting insights directly from people via interviews, surveys, and focus groups. Primary methods will be the most valuable for you because they're designed to answer specific questions about your customers and your business. For example, many companies have been switching to social media market research because social media and the internet have become so abundant in our society.

Many companies or individuals will post quick polls on their Instagram, Facebook, or Twitter feeds to get a quick response and gain popularity. Also, in these social media surveys, many people will vote and then comment on why they made this decision, giving companies or individuals greater, more in-depth feedback that can be used in the future. Polls and short surveys ultimately boost customer engagement, give crucial insights about a specific group, and create a persona for the intended audience.

Many companies these days are developing market research programs through their existing business practices. For example, Neil Patel asks for participation in a friendly onboarding survey for his search engine optimization tool.[5] Besides doing the dirty work to onboard a customer, he asks everyone who comes to the site to complete a survey. Not only does the survey information inform about how the product is made and refined, but the survey questions can and should provide insight into the changing demographics of your audience. The same applies to Noom, a dieting methodology.[6] Noom ask in-depth onboarding questions which find out about your weight, age, where you want to be, your habits, etc. If your market research is not part of your existing operations, you can certainly create surveys like the above.

Market testing or campaign effectiveness

Market testing is integral to online marketing. You should test your website's performance across multiple browsers and devices before launching it publicly. You can also run A/B tests to see what works best for your visitors. These tests help determine whether some aspects of your site work better than others. For example, one color scheme converts better.

Competitive analysis

A competitive analysis will usually choose a few of your significant rivals and analyze them for factors such as their overall strategy, customer perception, revenue or sales volumes, etc. Secondary sources such as newspaper reports, magazine features, and advertisements are good sources of competitive information. Still, primary investigations, such as mystery shopping or customer surveys, can provide valuable insights into customer service and current consumer opinion.

Consumer insights

Consumer insights are an essential part of any successful strategy. They reveal how people think, feel, and act, helping you understand them better so you can create products and services that resonate with them. Knowing your audience profoundly is essential to developing a strategic approach to your brand. Understanding your consumers' motivations, behaviors, and attitudes can lead to new product ideas, innovative advertising campaigns, and personalized experiences. Different types of consumer insight include qualitative (e.g. focus groups) and quantitative (e.g. surveys).

Voice of the customer

A voice of the consumer study is an online poll where consumers can rate their level of satisfaction with a product or company. Another popular method is called Net Promoter Score (NPS). In this case, companies pay a fee to receive feedback from current customers about whether they would recommend them to others. Companies then use these scores to gauge their success.

Segmentation

Segmentation in branding divides your market into distinct groups or segments based on shared characteristics such as values, beliefs, needs, aspirations, age, and gender. By understanding what differentiates each segment, companies can create marketing campaigns tailored to each group and maximize their appeal. Segmentation is important because it allows brands to be more focused and effective with their branding efforts by addressing the correct audience with relevant messages. Companies can build meaningful relationships with customers and foster loyalty among audiences by personalizing content for specific segments.

Gather information

This step is rooted deeply in the "identity" part of my methodology. This is where you look within and even back to find your roots and locate the emergence of each shred of your identity that drives the brand today.

I recommend starting with the past! As mentioned above, companies can use corporate history to celebrate achievements and inspire even greater things in the years ahead. It can help people learn about the company's origins and how they've grown into what they are today. In addition to preserving institutional knowledge, a corporate history also guides future leaders and managers. For example, if a company were to merge with another firm, having a detailed record of who was involved in the decision would be invaluable to the newly formed corporation.

In time, many companies lose track of why they were started in the first place, and if there isn't clear documentation of what you do, how you do it, and, most importantly, why you do it, it will be challenging to build on it. Market research is about understanding the marketing and communications messages, techniques, and channels to help you to define your breakthrough message and plan.

Do you wonder about your company's origin and its journey to success?

Investigating a company's origin gives us insights into industry trends and details about the start-up, such as its location, societal triggers at the time, initial consumers served, and the number of employees. By understanding how these have evolved, we can gain insight into the growth and success of the enterprise. Here are some questions to ask.

WHO STARTED THE COMPANY?
The first step in investigating a company's origin is to look for information about who started it. Usually, founders' names can be found on its website or in annual reports. Other sources include press releases or public records such as articles or investment round listings from sites like Crunchbase.

WHY WAS THE COMPANY STARTED?
Knowing why companies are started is key to understanding their origin story. To find out why a company was founded, try searching online for press releases announcing their product or service launch, which can provide clues about their founder's story for setting up

shop—though any bias needs to be considered when reading these stories. You can also look at what competitors were around then that might have been contributing factors in starting the business. This information usually comes from market analysis reports published by research firms.

WHAT DID THE COMPANY DO WHEN IT FIRST STARTED?

To get an idea of what the company did when it first began, search through news articles covering initial product demonstrations and customer reviews during its launch phase to learn more about additional features added over time as it grew and changed products, services, and teams throughout its lifespan. Additionally, interviews with founders may give insight into how they envisioned their original mission before all other external pressures later affected their business decisions.

WHERE WAS IT STARTED?

Tracing back where a company was first headquartered can provide an excellent starting point for your investigation into its founding story—even if it has moved locations multiple times since opening day!

WHAT WAS HAPPENING IN SOCIETY AT THE TIME THE COMPANY WAS FOUNDED? WERE THERE ANY TRIGGERS THAT PROMPTED ITS CREATION?

Taking a deeper dive into the historical context surrounding a particular business when it was founded is often crucial for getting a better understanding of why certain businesses came into existence and what other social phenomena may have indirectly influenced the company.

WHO DID THE COMPANY INITIALLY SERVE, AND HOW HAS THAT CHANGED OVER TIME?

Knowing the ideal audience at its early stages helps to inform more fully any subsequent changes motivated by changing audiences and products. Documents detailing backstory-related acquisitions could provide interesting evidence here, too; likewise, resources tracking consumer media buying decisions historically indicate changes being made within respective team rosters/roster composition responsible for taking care of logo promotion and actual message promotion itself.

HOW HAVE THINGS CHANGED SINCE THE COMPANY STARTED?

Understanding the changes in today's digital age since a company's start-up process is half the battle. Visiting media monitoring platforms such as Glassdoor and LinkedIn provides a window into past, present, and future market realities and customer interests, thus making it a much simpler task to find newsworthy items across varying industries. Using good old-fashioned sourced interview questions to find out about changes in mission/values, management style, product mix, employee count, store count, and budget can all point teams in the right direction, which they need in order to maintain their competitive edge out in the field.

When researching a company's origin, questions such as how many employees there were in year one, how many locations, and how profitable it was can provide helpful starting points. Additionally, delving into the specifics of how many products or services were initially sold and digging deeper into the type of promotion and related budget allocations at that time can also be helpful to trace a more thorough history. One should understand the message content used in advertising and budget allocation for promotional materials.

GATHER DATA FROM MULTIPLE SOURCES

Data collection has become increasingly important for successful personalization as technology has advanced. The goal is to make your data collection process comprehensive, nuanced, and user-friendly. An effective approach combines data collected from multiple sources such as surveys, online polls, website analytics programs, customer relationship management systems (CRMs), email subscriptions, and social media platforms.

ANALYZE THE DATA

Once your data is collected, it needs to be analyzed to determine patterns of behavior or beliefs so that you can tailor content towards specific groups of people.

UNDERSTAND PREFERENCES AND HABITS

To truly gain a deep understanding of an individual customer, you need to analyze more than just their demographic information, you also need to look at their preferences, habits, buying behavior, and likes/dislikes regarding products and services. This means collecting relevant information from surveys; tracking purchases through loyalty or rewards programs; analyzing web browsing behavior; tapping into analytics tools like heat maps or other behavioral indicators; conducting social listening initiatives; monitoring reviews across various channels; leveraging market research on competitive offerings; and getting feedback on promotions.

DISCOVER YOUR AUDIENCE

Creating a successful branding project relies heavily on understanding your audience. Doing the proper market research and leveraging the correct data can help you get to know your customers better, giving you the insights you need to craft a powerful brand narrative. Beyond just demographics, understanding their needs and wants allows you to create a tailored message unique to them. This will allow you to engage with them more meaningfully, helping you establish a trusted relationship between your brand and its audience.

ASSESS TONE

Look at their website copy, print ads, and social media content to develop an understanding of the tone of voice they use when engaging with prospects or customers. Companies tend to use more a formal tone when talking directly to prospective customers and a more casual tone on blogs or instructional pieces, so consider these differences when assessing the overall tone across different mediums. Additionally, note any humorous elements or competitive banter between them and other organizations to determine how they position themselves relative to competitors in the market.

ANALYZE COLORS AND FONTS

You might not think much about the fonts and colors used in advertisements, but these two elements convey certain feelings without having to say it outright in words. Each font has its style: for example, classic serif fonts can be seen as elegant or corporate depending on context; big chunky sans-serif fonts shout modern; comic sans font implies fun. Similarly with colors: red stimulates appetite, whereas green represents sustainability—so depending on your audience, brands need to pick font styles and color palettes appropriately for each type of demographic within their space.

Marketing research analysis

At this point, you can and should begin to document your research with the following frameworks:

- SWOT (strengths, weaknesses, opportunities, threats) analysis
- PESTEL analysis
- 5C analysis

SWOT

SWOT (strengths, weaknesses, opportunities, and threats) analysis, developed by business consultants in the early 1960s, is a valuable strategic management tool. A SWOT analysis investigates a brand's internal strengths and weaknesses as well as external opportunities and threats.[7] For a branding project, it can provide information about a brand that can help determine its potential success, which is why so many companies are turning to it when developing their strategies today. Using the SWOT analysis process, businesses can gain insight into their strengths and weaknesses, recognize opportunities they may not have taken advantage of in the past, and identify where new threats could come from in the future.

PESTEL analysis

Harvard professor Francis J. Aguilar first developed PESTEL analysis in the late 1960s. Organizations currently use it to identify and analyze the external marketing environment factors that may significantly impact their business, including political, economic, social, and technological forces. This strategic framework helps brands evaluate opportunities or threats in the external environment and make informed decisions on how to adjust their strategy accordingly. PESTEL analysis helps create a comprehensive picture of one's current business reality and allows companies to plan for future growth and success more accurately.[8]

POLITICAL FACTORS

PESTEL analysis for a business is essential to understanding the political factors that might impact decision-making. The political environment and regulatory policy have the potential to affect businesses significantly. A company needs to stay informed about the current political policies and their implications and look for possible opportunities in different markets.

ECONOMIC FACTORS

Regular reviews of economic factors allow companies to understand potential risks and optimize available resources and opportunities across different markets. Economic changes affect every business's performance, so it's important to assess these changes concerning consumers' buying power, market size, taxes, rates of growth or decline, etc. before making decisions that could enable future success or damage a business if the variables were overlooked.

SOCIAL FACTORS

A huge part of a successful PESTEL analysis includes researching social trends and acquiring customer insights. Fads come and go but staying informed on long-term values will help you identify long-term opportunities or needs that can be addressed more easily than short-term ones. Good customer research can yield extremely valuable information about customers, which can be used for marketing and product development purposes.

TECHNOLOGICAL FACTORS

Technology has had an increasing impact on businesses over recent years, so it makes sense to include this area in your PESTEL analysis too! Keeping up with technological developments enables your company to increase its efficiency, narrow its cost difference with competitor firms, and even become more attractive to foreign investors by creating attractive products based on new technology with less input cost! Therefore, assessing the rapidly changing technology scene can be key when conducting PESTEL analysis.

ENVIRONMENTAL FACTORS

Conducting PESTEL analysis must also include an external environmental scan of market-related events, such as weather conditions or other ecological disasters, which could temporarily disrupt operations geographically; it may even require you immediately to adopt certain strategies, etc. Doing this ensures compliance with environmental laws and regulations related to waste management, recycling, etc., thus enabling sustainable operating practices when applicable.

LEGAL FACTORS

An important factor when doing PESTEL analysis evaluations is considering legal implications such as financial laws, labor laws, antitrust laws, environmental laws, etc., because they often influence the degree of competition in the industry the firm is in; ignoring any implementation or reinforcement due to health and safety legislation could result in costly fines from governing bodies.

The 5C analysis

Have you ever heard of the 5C model? Another great approach, it adapts the Japanese strategist and corporate advisor Kenichi Ohmae's widely used 3C model for strategic management. Have you wondered what power or flexibility these two extra Cs bring? The 3C model has been widely adopted as a global company decision-making tool.

It considers three critical factors: customers, competitors, and the company's core competency, which decide the success of any business strategy for short-term or long-term goals. Now, by introducing two additional elements—context and collaborators—to create the 5C model, businesses can make more informed decisions which are likely to be more successful.[9]

CUSTOMER

When conducting a 5C analysis, the customer is the first C. Understanding your audience and their needs is essential to assess how best to meet them and ensure customer satisfaction. Consider your current consumers and any demographic segments that may be interested in your product or service. Uncovering customer preferences can provide invaluable insights into marketing strategies and product development, so thoroughly researching your ideal market is essential.

COMPETITION

The second C in a 5C analysis is competition. Evaluating competitors effectively will help you assess the competitive landscape, identify competitors, noting services/products offered as well as pricing, strengths, weaknesses, and promotional activities so you can benchmark yourself against them when developing strategies for opportunities for differentiation and getting ahead of the competition. Start by researching all existing successes.

COLLABORATORS

Collaboration is becoming increasingly important in today's business world, especially for small businesses looking to boost efficiency through partnerships or joint ventures with companies with complementary resources or expertise. Evaluating potential collaborators should involve consideration of both short-term objectives, such as cost-savings benefits from joint projects, and long-term opportunities, such as forming sustainable relationships with key partners.

CONTEXT

This refers to understanding the big picture—economic, political/legal, and technological—which will affect strategic decisions across all business areas, including operations, sales, marketing, etc. Considering market developments such as trends and seasonality is also part of context analysis but looking wider than just day-to-day operations can help realize growth opportunities which are more easily over-looked if analyzing specific parts in isolation only.

COMPANY

Finally, there's company analysis which considers internal factors like culture (ethics), staff skills, and capability, along with internal processes and systems used within the organization that impact its ability to succeed both now or in plans for expansion/new products, etc. Assessing company strengths and weaknesses plus overall agility levels (including scalability) will indicate readiness for achieving goals set, whether that involves responding quickly when tracking changes or handling increased demand due to planned growth activities/growth phases identified through competitor research previously referenced in the first C—customers.

In-depth interviews

An in-depth interview is a very effective way to get to know a person and understand how they think. In-depth interviews are a powerful tool to gain insights into how people perceive and experience products or services. When conducted correctly, they can be extremely beneficial for market researchers to understand their customer base better. Here's a list of steps for conducting in-depth interviews for market research.

1. Define the purpose of the interview

Before you start conducting in-depth interviews, you must determine what you want to learn from them. What issue(s) do you plan to explore with this research? What questions should you ask your participants? Most importantly, what story are you trying to uncover?

2. Choose your participants carefully

Once you set your goals, you'll need respondents who will answer your questions honestly and accurately. Aim for participants who represent your ideal demographic or may be exposed to similar marketing messages as your actual audience. Ensure the recruiters know exactly what type of person they should be looking for before beginning recruitment.

3. Create an interview guide

Rather than relying on spontaneous conversation, an interview guide is essential for setting up structured "conversations" that immediately dig into the core issues you need answers on. Don't let the conversation wander too far away from valuable information. A well-written interview prompter allows all participants and interviewers easy access to clear direction, giving each participant the same opportunity and consistency during each session.

CONVERSATIONAL GUIDE FOR INTERVIEWS

Objective: To determine the role of a website for a website redesign

Questions:

1 What role and key function should the website play for a company

   a. How can the website support cross-company initiatives?

   b. Is the website a valuable tool for driving the business, the brand, and the culture—if so, why? Or why not?

2 What types of digital activity would drive your business, and why?

3 What aspects of your website have the potential to be most valuable to your business? How could the website deliver return on investment (ROI) to your business?

Quantitative research often involves surveys, experiments, or statistical analysis. This approach allows researchers to collect, analyze, and interpret numerical results to conclude larger populations. Qualitative research, on the other hand, focuses on unstructured data such as opinions or experiences gathered through interviews and focus groups.

Keep digging

In 2009, when the world was amid a financial crisis, Uber and WhatsApp were founded. In 1975, Microsoft was born out of a recession. And in 2008, when the housing market crashed, Airbnb came into existence. What do all these companies have in common? They were founded during tough economic times by leaders who saw an opportunity during a crisis. So, if you're a leader looking to build something great, don't let a little (or a lot) of uncertainty stop you. The world needs your vision and your creativity now more than ever. It's time to step up and lead by example when it matters the most.

But if we look at the period when companies started and where companies are now, things are undoubtedly different. The world is unpredictable, and the one sure thing is things will change. If we revisit the answers to the questions you asked yourself about the past, especially if you were not a part of the company when you started, you might learn that the factors that led to the company being started have changed. You will also be able to see a vantage point that you would not be able to discover on the surface.

When Microsoft was first introduced, it was software you bought in a box. It had a disk and was installed on your computer. The cloud didn't exist. I remember when I used to save a document and send it, and everything stopped, and there were such version control issues. Then Google came along, and the social media age and collaboration tools like Slack and Microsoft needed to shift to keep up. But they were also not required to play catch-up; they needed to be ahead of the paradigm and constantly introduce new features, functionality, and value to the mix. They also needed to shift how they charge, and how people access their products, from one hefty fee to a much smaller and digestible price.

Here is a brainstorm of possible conversation starters for your interviews that will help you to get below the surface. Remember to ask why a lot and play devil's advocate to get to the core details you need to create a differentiated brand.

- Is the company today aligned with the reason why the company was started?
- Are there more locations and employees?
- How is the period we live in today different from when the company started?
- Has the company shifted based on the changing realities?
- How has the company changed based on the new facts?
- What new products, services, or offerings does the company now have? How many products or services did it use to sell?
- Have the new products or services enhanced the company and the value it drives?
- What is the current customer base? How has the customer base changed with time?
- Who does the company serve today? Is it different from who the company initially served?
- How have things changed since the company started?
- How has the company evolved over the years?
- How many employees are there now?
- How many locations does it now have?
- How has expansion enhanced the company's presence or detracted from it?
- What is the management structure?
- Is the company profitable now?
- How did the company promote itself?
- What is today's main message?

- What does advertising look like today? How has it shifted over time?
- What is your budget for advertising?
- Did all the changes enhance or detract?
- Is the original mission of the company intact?

Next, ask a current customer and a prospect the same questions. There is no need to do any fancy marketing study or to compensate people for this information. People are happy to help if they know why you are doing what you are doing and know that the information you are collecting will be used. A simple customized request on LinkedIn can lead to unexpected generosity. I have connected with many CMOs, entrepreneurs, and thought leaders at the top of their industries and companies. Many have invested time and freely shared ideas that can translate to a meaningful brand this way. And the best part about it is when you have a compelling conversation, that is just the beginning of a relationship.

Surveys help companies understand their market better by determining features and benefits that differentiate them from competitors. The findings are then translated into emotional customer-friendly terms. Surveys are one of the most effective ways to learn what consumers want. They're usually the only reliable method to get accurate results. Surveying people is one of the most effective ways to gather information about them. After all, the right questions can help you understand their needs better than anything else.

You don't need your market research department to conduct a brief survey, but at the same time, if you don't design the research properly, you may not get the information you need or the amount of information to make your research credible. Many survey tools like SurveyMonkey, Type form, and Qualtrics (an enterprise platform) make asking questions easy. They design them so that it does not feel like work for the person filling out the survey.

You may not need a survey. Don't survey if you already know the answer. If you're uncertain, you can informally ask people pointed questions to get your result. Because a survey of a few random people, especially people who are biased, will not give you definitive and scientifically valid results anyway.

Also, don't survey people and ask those less qualified than you to do your job. It bothers me to see all the surveys that happen as a company—name our new product (one you don't know about) for a $25 Starbucks gift card. What makes you think that with no information, education, or research, someone will come up with a better name than a professional who follows the methodical process? I am not saying that other opinions aren't valuable—they are—but, as you will learn through this chapter, it is critical to break down problems into small, attainable steps. In this case, what could you ask people, other than helping to come up with a name for a product they don't know about?

- You can run three ideas of names by your panel
- You can do a focus group to define names
- You can do some fun exercises where you share pictures and figures and ask what comes to mind

Ultimately if you give away the strategic moments of being a marketer to untrained and unappreciative people, it will continue to degrade respect for our profession. On top of that, marketing is a system of intricate pieces and parts that must come together. You are the architect, and you can't just wing it or delegate it to an uninformed novice and expect to get your desired outcome.

Organize, interpret, and analyze data

In the modern age, companies have access to more data than ever before. This data can help them gain insights into their business operations and make better-informed decisions. However, to use this data to its fullest potential, organizations need to ensure that they have the proper structure and processes in place.

Before you begin using data for insights and decisions, it is essential to set clear success metrics. Without explicitly established metrics of victory, it will be difficult to determine if a decision was successful or not. It is also essential to involve cross-functional teams when setting these metrics as different stakeholders might have different perspectives about what constitutes success for a given project or goal.

Once you've established what your measures of success are, it's time to create a data infrastructure that can make collecting and analyzing this information easier. This often means investing in the right systems—hardware and software that enable agile access to bigger databases with more granular information; think AI or automation platforms that eliminate tedious manual input tasks while enabling faster processing times.

Have you ever considered the differences between data, information, knowledge, and wisdom? Knowing these concepts can be necessary for working with systems that collect immense amounts of data.

The concepts of data, information, knowledge, and wisdom have been explored for centuries. However, the groundbreaking work of Dr. Russell Ackoff revolutionized how we think about this field. His theories have been applied in various contexts and have helped improve systems within many organizations, from corporate offices to police departments. Ultimately, Dr. Ackoff's work continues to prove invaluable when attempting to identify business growth opportunities and gain efficient customer-focused solutions for long-term success.[10]

The combination of these four interconnected factors is becoming increasingly important for decision-making in business and branding and nearly any other domain or application. In an age where technology can provide immense amounts of information at our fingertips swiftly and accurately, understanding how these factors are connected is becoming more integral.

Data is often equated to bright ideas and positive results, but it's not quite as simple as collecting a few numbers and getting a useful insight. To maximize the potential from data-driven insights, it is necessary to understand what separates data, information, knowledge, and wisdom. In doing so, it is possible to go beyond collecting data and use this information to create meaningful recommendations. You can make the most of their data-driven insights by understanding the difference between these four major concepts and turning them into actionable steps.

Analyzing your current data is the first step in making the most of your data-driven insights. What type of data are you collecting and gathering? Is it quantitative or qualitative? Are there any biases or inaccuracies in your existing dataset? Consider all aspects of your collected data before moving on to the next step.

Once you've assessed your collected data, you need to transform it into information that can be used for decisions or recommendations. This transformation takes more than just some algebraic equations; instead, it requires understanding the bigger picture behind the numbers, identifying patterns in the dataset, tying unrelated elements together—all while monitoring accuracy throughout the process.

Once you have sound information available from your dataset, it's then time to apply knowledge to make sense of these facts and draw meaningful conclusions based on them—such as creating customer profiles or segmenting users with similar preferences—which in turn helps build wisdom (or learning) regarding in what direction an organization should take its marketing campaigns or strategies in the future.

Create an environment that leads to recommendations

When leveraging data for business decisions, it isn't just the size of the datasets that matters, it's what an organization does with it. Businesses should strive to be innovative when collecting, organizing, and utilizing their raw numbers—thinking beyond traditional reporting metrics into more complex questions.

Dashboards help to arrange data. With most technical dashboard software, you can integrate all marketing activities into one cohesive funnel without manipulating multiple systems. Such dashboards make it possible to see web analytics, count attendees at live events, and checked-out tickets from different systems promptly. For instance, whenever we carry out a campaign, we can observe multiple-colored gauges. If something is labeled red, we can take remedial action through various marketing sources and check its effect immediately.

Another essential tip for unlocking maximum value from big data is leveraging visualization tools such as interactive dashboards which allow businesses to quickly glean insights from vast amounts of information in meaningful ways, so they don't get overwhelmed by raw numbers but instead focus on actionable results based on these insights.

Understanding customer trends and behaviors is key to successful business decisions and operations. Collecting customer data through market research, surveys, and other sources provides businesses with actionable insights, which can then be used to create strategies that result in increased operational efficiencies or product launches. Automation technologies like Zapier or IFTTT can help streamline marketing analytics capabilities by linking multiple marketing and CRM systems as well as automating workflows. By leveraging these types of automation tools, businesses can gain powerful insights from their datasets more quickly and efficiently than ever before.

Data democratization: Unlocking the power of data for your brand

Quality decision-making is paramount for any business, regardless of its size or complexity. Data democratization can help businesses gain access to reliable sources of information about products, customers, and markets that allow them to make more informed decisions faster. By having unfettered access to robust datasets, you are able not just to act quickly but also to protect against risks associated with poor decisions.

Without access to the same sources of data, departments within an organization can easily fall into siloed systems where they are unable to find common ground on which strategies have been built and implemented. With increased access across all levels of the organization available both internally and remotely, it's easier for employees to communicate using trusted sources as a reference point when discussing different topics or objectives. This more effective collaboration improves customer engagement and satisfaction too, thanks to improved clarity on issues being discussed.

With everyone in your organization having equal access to the same information, you're provided with opportunities and insights that otherwise would be lost due to limited accessibility. Being able to explore new ideas as well as fine-tune strategies for different customer segments leads the way for remarkable internal and external collaborations which could otherwise be difficult due to varying degrees of expertise among those involved. Additionally, increased understanding of how best to interpret available data leads companies down paths that were elusive before advances in data democratization practices were introduced!

YOUR RECOMMENDATIONS

Here are some tips for writing market research recommendations.

Develop recommendations that solve problems

The most successful recommendations come from taking an issue or set of problems and developing solutions that solve those problems. It would be best if you tied the findings from all areas of your research—including but not limited to surveys, focus groups, interviews, etc.—into a unified set of solutions that will help resolve any issues related to the project or institution at hand.

Be specific and actionable when writing recommendations

Recommendations should be specific enough so that anyone reading it knows when, where, how, and why they need to act for their business or organization to succeed. Avoid using marketing jargon and acronyms; provide clear steps for moving forward with each recommendation.

Ensure recommendations go hand in hand with your research insights

Make sure every recommendation is linked back—either directly or indirectly—to one or more insights from your overall market research effort. Doing this will ensure maximum impact from each recommendation presented in terms of accuracy and useful application within an organization's decision-making process.

Provide clear evidence for each recommendation

Strong recommendations derive power from competent evidence gathered through robust data analysis efforts. If there are practical considerations behind one of your findings (for example, cost/benefit analysis), make sure these reasons are clearly outlined as well if it helps support the validity of the recommendation being proposed.

From insights to recommendations

Organizational transformation can be a daunting prospect. It's hard to know what will work, and many people fear the risk of making significant changes. But with the proper research and drive towards progress, it is possible to achieve meaningful organizational change.

When faced with any issue or problem, it is essential to look at what exactly needs resolving and identify all the components that need tackling. By putting together a chart of these critical elements, you can begin breaking down the problem into smaller chunks and determining how they contribute to the overall cause-and-effect structure. Furthermore, these visuals can assist in outlining goals and understanding how each element interacts within the context of other factors to arrive at a successful resolution.

When you lead a branding project, especially in larger multinational companies, it's crucial to understand corporate ecosystems, how cross-functional teams interact, and the critical elements for alignment and integration. To address these challenges, my friend and colleague David Berenbroick and I set out to develop a proprietary model of corporate ecosystems that features circles representing different functions and how they interact.[11]

Our goal through this model is to introduce a new understanding of the possible holes and opportunities available within the corporate structure. The model aims to show how you can adopt a transformational and branding project that is all-encompassing and not isolated to your department or function. In aiming for collective achievement, we aim to bridge the gap between individual teams whose objectives might overlap or go against each other's intentions. With this proposed model, our goal is to provide an expansive view of potential changes and outcomes within your organization.

By conducting in-depth interviews with stakeholders across the organizations, our research process uncovered key areas for growth opportunities that still needed to be identified. This process allowed us to gain a better understanding of their current state and anticipate potential challenges that may arise during implementation or execution. It also helped us realize any blind spots in our strategy or plans, thus empowering us to better prepare for those challenges and take advantage of opportunities.

The underlying idea behind our model is that in authentically integrating corporate systems, you must consider all functions involved: product, engineering, marketing, but also finance, operations, legal, customer support, and more (anyone who interacts with your customers or products). Each of these functions should be able to speak from their own perspectives based on job-specific context as well as shared context gained from working with other areas; however, if any one or two circles ignore the others then gaps will emerge between strategy and execution resulting in disappointed customers. Ultimately each area needs complete visibility into multiple levels: users' experiences in real time, a bigger picture view of performance over time, and potential problems or unexpected successes at every corner.

Many companies get caught up in individual teams competing for resources instead of building collectively towards shared success; but without proper integration between business units, major projects will fail as they become lost in translation or move forward too slowly when accountability isn't clear. To ensure lasting change happens cross-functionally requires building bridges between siloes by listening deeply and creating processes that encourage collaboration. A digital transformation roadmap must consider both the stakeholders' need for executional speed as well as strategic visioning conversations allowing them to tap into employee creativity while providing guard rails through which product innovations can be explored without breaking budget limits or risk assessment parameters.

We made deliberate choices in how to display this information. Circles effectively represent data, enabling organizations to interpret better systems and behaviors that would otherwise go unseen. Circles allow for a more holistic approach to organizational management, enabling businesses to quickly adapt to unknown environmental elements instead of relying on rigid models. Additionally, circles allow for new organizational opportunities by providing avenues for members to communicate more effectively and strategize around contingencies more accurately. By using circles over linear models, organizations can gain reliable insights to achieve success faster, no matter what unexpected changes occur.

It's important to prepare a report that highlights key trends and tells a story about how specific measures relate back to each other within a given context. A good way of doing this is to create visuals like infographics which provide easy mechanisms for conveying complex information and allow stakeholders who don't have analytics backgrounds to get quickly oriented with insights made possible through collected data sets.

Organizations can tap into untapped potential by understanding how to combine research and innovation by uncovering deeply rooted beliefs and assumptions. With new insights, production processes can be improved, unlocking hidden advantages and initiatives which could lead to improved customer experiences. It's essential to recognize the long-term commitment these projects will require, with executives rarely staying for more than three years. For that reason, collaboration is essential—bringing stakeholders together to work towards mutual goals should help facilitate user experience improvements across multiple systems.

Show and tell

Market intelligence is a powerful tool for developing strategies, leveraging opportunities, and revealing changes in your clients' industry. However, presenting clients with a finished report covering market research can leave them feeling disconnected from the process. Sharing the progression behind your findings gives stakeholders insight into how marketing projects came together and keeps them invested throughout.

Market intelligence does not end once findings are communicated back but becomes instead part of a continuous cycle aimed at helping organizations stay ahead by empowering strategic decision-makers with reliable insights.

Gauge and measure attainable goals

It's time to break your long-term goals into achievable chunks and optimize your potential. Objectives and key results (OKRs) are the

FIGURE 9.1

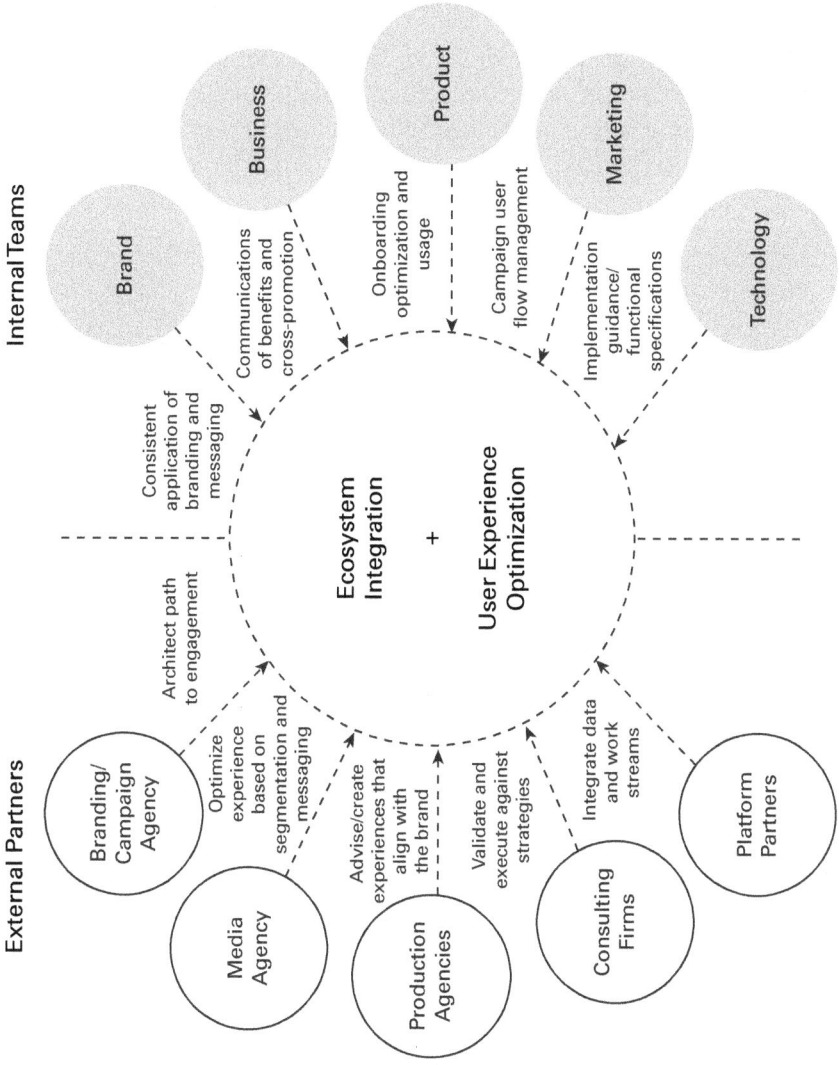

External Partners

Internal Teams

Branding/Campaign Agency

Media Agency

Production Agencies

Consulting Firms

Platform Partners

Brand

Business

Product

Marketing

Technology

Ecosystem Integration
+
User Experience Optimization

Consistent application of branding and messaging

Communications of benefits and cross-promotion

Onboarding optimization and usage

Campaign user flow management

Implementation guidance/functional specifications

Architect path to engagement

Optimize experience based on segmentation and messaging

Advise/create experiences that align with the brand

Validate and execute against strategies

Integrate data and work streams

most powerful way of setting and achieving attainable goals.[12] OKRs were introduced by Andy Grove, former CEO of Intel, who believed that organizations should set their standards for measuring success. An OKR is a statement of direction (or objective) paired with measurable outcomes (key results). The objectives should be ambitious but realistic; they signal ownership, determination, and guidance, while key results provide evidence typically backed by numbers indicating whether a given pursuit has been successful or not.

OKRs identify exactly what the user needs to accomplish on an individual level or as a whole organization. With these results set up, one can quickly identify the progress needed for completion, rearrange tasks if required priority-wise, and track progress on any project throughout its life cycle. In this way, every facet of your business plan becomes accountable for measurable performance indicators—resulting in better strategic planning with greater efficiency. Besides this, teams that use OKRs benefit from improved communication between stakeholders and greater clarity in organizational objectives across all levels of business operations.

Creating practical OKRs requires careful thought to bring out maximum efficiency from the activities involved.

Step 1—Define your objective

An OKR outlines what success looks like and helps teams understand which efforts matter most in the pursuit of that success. It focuses on measurable results, not daily tasks, and should be allowed to evolve over time as demands change. Setting specific goals and tracking whether they have been met helps maintain focus on the important things throughout an organization, project or initiative. Additionally, OKRs help foster a greater understanding between team members since everyone is aware of and actively working towards the same set of objectives. Tracking and measuring progress is particularly useful for understanding which tactics are driving success and allows leaders to focus resources where they'll have the most impact.

- Example: Launch a new digital product

Step 2—Break it down into manageable pieces: set specific key results

Once you have defined the objective, it's time to set specific key results (KRs). These are measurable indicators of progress that help track performance towards the stated objective in detail.

- Example: If your objective is "Increase brand visibility by 10%," then some key results could include:
  - Complete development within 4 months
  - Reach 10,000 users in the first quarter
  - Achieve 20% user retention rate after 6 months

Step 3—Develop an implementation plan

It is time to break down the KRs into a timeline and implementation plan. Through this process, you can allocate resources and assign tasks accordingly so that everyone involved in the project knows when they need to complete their assigned tasks.

- Example: Complete development within 4 months

To do this, follow the steps below.

Prepare an initial timeline: Before jumping into the project and attempting to meet a deadline, it's essential to have a clear roadmap or timeline of what tasks need to be completed, who will handle them, and in what order they will be done. Without this kind of overview, it is challenging to ensure that dates are met and that nothing is missed along the way.

Utilize a project management tool: Project management tools are invaluable for staying on track with your development projects. These tools offer features like task lists and Gantt charts that track the progress the team is making towards their goals. They also help break down complex tasks into smaller portions that can be more easily managed by allowing you to assign each portion with its own deadlines or due date requirements.

Plan regular meetings: Meetings give teams an opportunity to share their ideas as well as coordinate action plans in order to move forward on projects in a timely manner. Regular check-ins and updates allow teams to identify any issues early on in the process, giving them enough time to course-correct before falling too far behind schedule.

Set realistic milestones: The best way for a team to stay focused and motivated during lengthy projects is by setting achievable goals that lead to completing the entire thing one step at a time within the targeted time frame. Breaking it down into smaller chunks makes it easier for everyone involved so no one gets overwhelmed with too much at once or discouraged if small hurdles arise along the way.

Identify risks quickly: Risks are expected when new development projects are undertaken. Every team should have a plan for how they will be dealt with should they arise during their project window since unexpected developments can lead to significant delays if not addressed sooner rather than later. The best method here is keeping an open line of communication between all parties involved; this allows decisions to be made quickly when issues occur, helping keep everything running smoothly and ensuring deadlines can still be met even when there are surprises.

Develop contingency plans: In addition, having several backup plans in place when something goes wrong gives teams peace of mind knowing they won't fall too far behind should something unexpected pop up while working towards their completion goal. Additionally, teams can look back after each round of work completed, learn from any mistakes made, and review how processes were handled so future projects become more efficient overall by avoiding similar problems in the future thanks to the past experience from this project complete methodology.

Step 4—Track progress regularly

The purpose of using OKRs in a branding context is to ensure that all team members are working towards achieving tangible, meaningful results. OKRs can provide structure and clarity to the development process while considering available resources, forecasting scenarios, and workforce capabilities. When creating OKRs, it is essential to define objectives that reflect the desired outcome and set goals that detail how these objectives will be achieved. Additionally, meaningful criteria must be established to ensure success during the implementation phase, leading towards timely realizations of results through cumulative growth and trust. With effective OKR processes in place for branding projects, teams can measure their progress against realistic benchmarks and strive for continuous improvement towards achieving the desired outcome. Here's how to do this:

Set up infrastructure: The first step to achieving these ambitious goals is setting up the necessary infrastructure, including hosting, databases, APIs, and more. Working closely with developers is essential to ensure everything is set up and running optimally. Properly utilizing tools such as DevOps and Infrastructure as Code (IaC) can help make this process easier.

Create a product roadmap: Understanding what features you want to develop and when will be vital for completing development. Creating a product roadmap can give everyone involved with the project visibility into what needs to be accomplished and when it needs to be done. Setting achievable mini-goals along the way will also help keep everyone on track while working towards the larger goal of completing development in four months.

Use analytics tools to track progress: Analytics tools are essential for measuring progress towards goals like user retention rate and the number of new customers acquired each quarter. Utilizing analytics tools will allow you to track how well your campaigns perform so you can adjust your strategies accordingly for maximum impact.

Stay organized and communicate effectively: For these ambitious goals to be achieved efficiently and in order to stay organized, team members should always remain in close communication.

Step 5—Assess outcomes and track progress regularly

You can track OKRs regularly using KPIs like revenue growth rate or website traffic increase percentage, which give you factual data regarding how close you are to achieving success with your branding project. Once the key results have been achieved, take time to properly assess what worked and didn't work so that you can do things better and more efficiently next time.

OKRS: A FEW SIMPLE GUIDELINES TO KEEP IN MIND

Less is more

You might feel the urge to include more and more pointers in your list, but it is better to keep your OKRs to between three and five per cycle. This will keep you from getting overwhelmed.

Stay flexible

Pushing yourself to your limit is good, but it should not make you feel incapable. If an objective or KR seems irrelevant, get rid of it.

Dare to fail

People achieve more when their goals require them to grow beyond their current capability, so sometimes, failing to meet your goals is okay. You will locate your weaknesses that way.

Be patient

This is a process, and trial and error is your friend. You will do it poorly before you do it with excellence, so have faith in yourself and persevere![13]

The three questions "what," "how," and "why" form the blueprint of a plan and the creation of an attainable goal, so make sure yours is well-detailed and executable. If you start and end with these questions, your arrows consistently point you towards success. Once you know how to measure your goals, you'll already be on your way to achieving them.

Marketers need to focus on where they are headed and need to be less concerned about how long it will take for someone to get to their destination. While a marketer may understand the person better than they understand themselves, the person needs to own the decision to engage and needs to do it in their own time. In my experience, a lot of my clients reach out to me many months after I've reached out to them. I am totally okay with that because if I do my marketing right, then people will be reaching out to me several months after I've reached out to them on an ongoing basis, and that's what I need to have an entire pipeline of customers.

Endnotes

1 American Anthropological Association (nd) What is anthropology?, americananthro.org/AdvanceYourCareer/Content.aspx?ItemNumber=2150 (archived at https://perma.cc/2VRE-BZRC)

2 Genest, J (2022, July 27) Problem statement framing, *Investigations of a Dog*, investigationsquality.com/2021/05/23/problem-statement-framing (archived at https://perma.cc/N5EJ-Z4RL)

3 Mandel, J (2022, December 22) Interview with Jon Yanovsky. Used with permission

4 allBusiness (nd) 5 basic methods of market research, allbusiness.com/the-five-basic-methods-of-market-research-1287-1.html (archived at https://perma.cc/6Y82-9D9W)

5 Patel, N (2023, January 16) Ubersuggest: Free keyword research tool, Neil Patel, neilpatel.com/ubersuggest/ (archived at https://perma.cc/Q7D8-P6WC)

6 Noom, noom.com/ (archived at https://perma.cc/Q7D8-P6WC)

7 White, J (2022, May 11) What is a SWOT analysis?, *Forbes*, forbes.com/advisor/business/what-is-swot-analysis/ (archived at https://perma.cc/HW94-BHHZ)

8 Peterdy, K (2022, November 24) PESTEL Analysis, Corporate Finance Institute, corporatefinanceinstitute.com/resources/management/pestel-analysis/ (archived at https://perma.cc/33H4-TLEQ)

9 CFI Team (2022, December 1) 5C Analysis, Corporate Finance Institute, corporatefinanceinstitute.com/resources/management/5c-analysis-marketing (archived at https://perma.cc/WQG7-FZ69)

10 Bernstein, J H (nd) The data-information-knowledge-wisdom hierarchy and its antithesis, journals.lib.washington.edu/index.php/nasko/article/download/12806/11288/0 (archived at https://perma.cc/26EG-67B8)

11 Berenbroik, D and Mandel, J (2022, February 2) Spider Chart

12 What Matters (nd) What is an OKR? Definition and examples, www.whatmatters.com/faqs/okr-meaning-definition-example (archived at https://perma.cc/4NGU-XUBX)

13 Mandel, J (2022, May 6) Gauge and measure attainable goals with these 3 metrics, Lifehack, lifehack.org/893088/attainable-goals (archived at https://perma.cc/E9SP-PGZ9)

10

Your Company's Movement

Businesses need to help someone get from where they are to where they need to go. Marketers are the ones to champion this. Whether your audience is looking for a car, a strategic consulting engagement, or a diet, they spend their valuable time and money to get somewhere they can't or don't believe they can on their own. Whether it entails creating jobs in developing countries, finding a solution for an environmental issue, providing access to essential services for those in need, or simply making it easier to recycle something, a movement should have a lasting impact on society and make a difference in people's lives.

A clear sense of direction is essential when navigating through the early stages of launching a business or pushing onward in an existing venture. And the good news is that we've spent so much time asking many questions about where your company is, where your company is going, and who works there that we're already close to our answer.

Let's say you work at a large company with a history of growth through acquisition, technology, or innovation, and you have an account of all the issues addressed. Earlier in the book, we discussed performative allyship, which means jumping on the bandwagon without a solid understanding of how you will support the issue. If you find your company jumping from campaign to campaign without a clear stake in the ground, it is time to define your movement.

The "identity" portion covered in the first section of this book sets the foundation for having a crystal-clear vision of who you are. Next, the "intention" for your brand will help you create focus and meaning around that brand identity for yourself and the company. Once you realize and form your business identity, you must meticulously strategize how you will approach your customers on your platform. This brings in the process of "implementation." In this stage, you're focusing on that final touchpoint with consumers—the most visible piece. It could be your website, a social media handle, or a physical presence.

Purpose and values are essential to a business or individual, but that purpose can easily be forgotten without a movement. A movement takes your purpose and values and raises awareness to ensure that people know what you do, why you do it, and how they can join. When creating a movement, ensure that your purpose is at the core of it. The purpose should be communicated so everyone understands what you are trying to achieve. This will ensure that everyone who joins in on the action shares the same vision and beliefs as you, making collaboration more effective.

In today's ever-evolving workplace, fostering a movement and community based on authentic beliefs and principles is becoming increasingly popular among employers. By doing this, they can drive employees, give them meaningful purpose within the organization, raise morale, create an action plan that aligns with their values, and provide superior service and results to consumers.

The mind of a meaningful marketer is focused on analytics, instinct, and creativity. A successful digital marketer must understand traditional marketing principles and modern technology. You need to be able to use your experience and knowledge in combination with data-driven decision-making to craft effective campaigns.

When crafting campaigns, if they want them to stand out from their competition marketers need a creative spark—the willingness or ability to apply knowledge inventively rather than merely laying down established practices or principles reliably but unimaginatively. Innovative thinking can help marketers stay ahead of the curve by introducing novel ways for their customer base to engage with their brand online through interactive experiences that attract potential customers while fostering existing relationships at the same time. In addition, by combining analytics with creativity over time, marketers can get an increasingly accurate understanding of current customer wants and needs on every channel they use, increasing engagement overall and improving loyalty and customer returns.

This chapter will discuss how to display those answers to give you an inspiring narrative and movement for your company. Purpose gives companies and customers a reason to continue striving forward even when times are tough—it keeps them motivated through difficult situations because they have something to keep working towards that has actual value outside of profitability. But not all companies have the luxury of inventing a story from the beginning. This chapter is strategically placed after the previous chapter on market research. Research is essential for a successful brand because it enables them to identify and understand customer needs, wants, and feelings. Connecting this research with the techniques mentioned in this chapter helps to ensure that the marketing strategies and actions taken are grounded.

Movements are not campaigns

It is often hard to discern the difference between a movement and a campaign. The language around them is often used interchangeably, making it difficult to distinguish their approaches and understand their purpose. Though they share similar goals, campaigns often have finite objectives, while movements pursue societal changes over time. When it comes to making a real difference in society, the choice between starting a movement or a campaign can be difficult. Nevertheless, it is essential to distinguish between them because they have different objectives and approach their goals differently.

Campaigns are short-term initiatives with specific goals. To implement these goals via the campaign, you often have a predetermined, limited set of resources available for use. These focus on achieving set outcomes within an established period and involve activities such as advertising, media placements, events, and protests through highly focused efforts that reach a defined audience.

Movements involve longer-term pursuits of large-scale societal changes that may extend beyond the boundaries of a single campaign or initiative and even beyond what your company does and how it is done. Unlike campaigns, movements don't usually have defined tasks or timelines; instead, they advocate for systemic change in areas such as civil rights, healthcare, gender equality, or education reform by engaging people to participate over long periods with ongoing recruitment efforts designed to build momentum and engage more advocates over time.

Though both require energy and resources, movements lead to profound cultural transformation. In contrast, campaigns often equate to fleeting attention around an issue intended to influence policy and decisions within windows of only a few months. Moreover, movements tend to be less structured, and their impact is much harder to quantify than campaigns which use metrics such as "likes" and "followers" as proof of success when effective communication across multiple channels has been established.

Ultimately, each approach should be tailor-made based on individual needs according to research about the audience(s), duration of desired impact, and statements about expected results from selected strategies ahead of budget constraints being taken into consideration, if resources allow. The building blocks used might look similar but depending on overall goals, whether you opt for launching either a campaign or a movement will depend mainly upon those factors above, where each could bring about lasting change if successful, so take your time finding what works best for the situation at hand!

Embody and promote your company's values: Start with your company's movement

Engaging in a movement can help brands foster customer loyalty. By showing that your business supports causes important to your audience, you are cultivating an emotional connection between the customer and your business. It would be best if you cared about the same things as your customers. By participating in a movement, you are also sending out a message that tells your customers that when they purchase from you, their money will benefit people (or the planet) in some way, which can be incredibly powerful.

A well-implemented movement not only generates awareness around your brand but can also boost your brand identity—allowing you to stand out from competitors and attract potential new customers. As well as helping build relationships with existing customers and potential new ones, participating in a movement can also create an authentic story for your business, where people understand who you are and what kind of impact you want to make on the world.

Companies like Nike, Dove, and Absolute Vodka often have movements and associated campaigns congruent with their causes. This provides a more significant impact than randomly advertising products, features, and functions. I will share case studies later in this chapter that show how their campaigns connect to their overarching movements. Furthermore, the movements and stories these companies tell are based on deep histories that a company can support.

A movement allows businesses to try out different strategies—from launching groundbreaking products or services to experimenting with new advertising campaigns—all of which help generate customer feedback on how successful specific initiatives were and how best to move forward. This helps businesses refine their approach over time to resonate better with their audiences.

Movements offer businesses plenty of opportunities, including fostering customer loyalty, attracting more customers, and building brand identity while creating positive social change, something everyone should strive towards achieving regardless of the industry they're in!

The success of a social movement depends on having the right mix of an emotional message, effective tactics, and strong leadership. As a result, social movements are becoming increasingly important for marketers as an industry that increasingly recognizes the value placed on emotional engagement.

Initiating a movement includes turning a belief into an issue that strikes a chord with a particular audience. So, let's delve into Sweetgreen as a present-day enterprise and movement, creating a model for connecting purpose with passion and what customers want.

THE FOUNDING OF SWEETGREEN

Sweetgreen is a fast-growing, sustainable restaurant chain that has brought healthy eating options to thousands of customers across the United States and around the world. Founded in 2007, it quickly gained popularity for its focus on healthy ingredients and commitment to sustainability. Today, we're going to explore the Sweetgreen story, from its humble beginnings to its incredible success.

In 2007, Nicolas Jammet, Jonathan Neman, and Nathaniel Ru started Sweetgreen; just a couple of months after college graduation, their first location was a tiny suburban Washington, DC space. They had an established goal: bring fresh and nutritious food to their community.

After gaining initial success within their local region, they raised $22 million with high-profile investors such as Jeremiah Simons (founder of Panera Bread). This allowed them to expand rapidly, and at the time of writing they have nearly 200 locations across the United States and several locations worldwide.[1]

Recent acquisitions and expansion

Sweetgreen invested in Dig Inn (now known as Dig), an urban farm-to-counter restaurant chain specializing in seasonal ingredients sourced regionally. They also recently acquired greenGOES tech, a goal-oriented app that provides consumers with nutritional information tailored to their fitness goals. These investments open new potential and allow Sweetgreen to continue growing while maintaining its commitment to providing healthier options at affordable prices.

Environmental impact

The Sweetgreen operations are marketed as climate conscious: for example, offering compostable packaging and energy-efficient systems, including energy usage data tracking. Sweetgreen has firmly established itself as a strong advocate for sustainable business models whose operations aim at creating a lower environmental impact, even signing the New Plastics Economy Pledge in June 2020.[2]

As a socially responsible business, Sweetgreen has taken many steps to build an environmental brand purpose. It has been dedicated to sourcing and serving local food products and creating sustainable business strategies. However, as the company grows, its actions must align with these core values, promoting its products and connecting them to its overarching purpose. Beyond that, their influence reaches out into the community, with support for local charities and organizations and initiatives that build trust with stakeholders. This effort reflects a passionate dedication to making a real difference in people's lives.

But what if your business needs to be established? Creating a movement for your company or you can be a sweet dream come true but it can also be overwhelming at first. Creating a movement is about tapping into yours and your company's shared values and beliefs which unites people and groups in pursuit of common goals. It's about setting an ambitious goal and inspiring others to join in.

Your organization may feel overwhelming or too complicated to navigate. Or maybe you don't have complete autonomy over the marketing department? If so, your best bet may be to start with a campaign and work your way up to a movement. This approach can help focus efforts on achieving specific goals while simultaneously building support and appeal for long-term objectives.

Leverage successful case studies as a source of knowledge

As a marketer, it is essential to recognize that the modern consumer has ever-evolving demands and needs. To do so, you must identify the needs of your customer base and know exactly what their dreams and desires are. Once these have been identified, you must create a custom solution to satisfy them. Meaningful marketing and branding requires forging genuine relationships with potential customers to earn their trust and business. It would be best to show that your product or service could offer them the most value and provide solutions.

Using real-world case studies can be an effective way for small businesses to build successful marketing plans or improve existing processes. By studying how others have achieved success within the industry, businesses can gain invaluable insights into practices that worked well and those they should avoid altogether while building their strategy. However, there are some key things to remember when leveraging case studies. First, even though an organization may have achieved its goal in a relatively short time due to experience or knowledge in the field, new businesses should set realistic expectations for themselves about how quickly goals could be met without prior expertise in digital marketing strategy implementation. Second, commitment is vital—success takes time! It is essential to keep up with industry trends while implementing tactics over extended periods if one intends on maximum returns on investments now and into the future. Finally, don't forget that learning isn't something that should stop once a plan has been implemented; continued growth is possible through understanding advantages over competitors while creating lasting impressions with ultimate customer loyalty now and in the future!

Nike's Dream Crazier campaign[4]

- Attributes: daring, innovative, bold
- Ethos: Nike is about pushing yourself to reach your greatest potential and to strive for the impossible. With daring innovation, we explore new boundaries in order to help you reach your goals
- Slogan/movement: "Just Do It"

Nike released its "Dream Crazier" commercial on International Women's Day in 2019. The campaign was created to inspire and empower women worldwide, encouraging them to strive for greatness despite their daily challenges. The powerful commercial features narration by tennis star Serena Williams and has received hugely positive feedback from viewers around the globe.

The campaign was effective because it appealed to people's emotions by empowering them and inspiring them to act. It communicated a powerful message to its audience that everyone can achieve their dreams, no matter how crazy they may seem. Additionally, the ad's compelling visuals and upbeat music helped create a positive and motivational atmosphere, encouraging people to break barriers and achieve their ambitions.

Dove's Real Beauty Sketches campaign[5]

- Attributes: gentle, nourishing, caring
- Ethos: Dove believes in empowering people to feel more beautiful daily. Our products help women recognize and appreciate their unique beauty
- Slogan/movement: "Let your beauty shine"

Dove released their groundbreaking "Real Beauty Sketches" video in 2013, which highlighted women's perceptions about themselves compared to perceptions from strangers—resulting in a greater appreciation for natural beauty rather than stereotypes perpetuated by social media standards. Dove has continued with similar campaigns over the years, consistently reinforcing their message that beauty comes in many forms and can be found within all individuals no matter what shape or size you may be.[6]

The campaign was effective for the brand because it tapped into women's emotions, reminding them that they are beautiful no matter their shape or size. Moreover, by focusing on real people rather than models, the campaign normalized beauty and created a conversation between people about media representation and beauty ideals. The fact that Dove shared positive stories that could resonate with viewers made it more relatable and memorable, contributing to its success.

Absolut Vodka Pride bars and lounges campaign[7]

- Attributes: absolute, pure, timeless
- Ethos: Absolut stands for absolute quality and style. We strive for the purest spirit to be shared with timeless appeal
- Slogan: "Absolut perfection"

Absolut Vodka launched its #RainbowInside global pride campaign to show their commitment to LGBTQ+ community rights and equal representation through social media channels and urban Rainbow Pride bars and lounges set up throughout various cities in Europe during Pride Month 2019. So far, there have been unique lounges decorated with colorful rainbow flags in Madrid, Barcelona, Paris, and Amsterdam, bringing together people from communities all over Europe to celebrate diversity under one roof.

The Absolut Vodka Pride bars and lounges campaign was effective for the brand due to its focus on appealing to a specific demographic, namely the LGBTQ+ community. The campaign acknowledged and celebrated the individuals featured in the previous campaigns and highlighted their stories, lending visibility and inclusivity to all queer-identifying people. Additionally, the partnership with various LGBTQ+ organizations allowed those organizations to receive funding and gain valuable exposure. By authentically engaging with the LGBTQ+ community, the campaign increased brand loyalty while providing meaningful connections that fostered a sense of belonging.

PROMOTE YOUR INITIATIVE AND YOURSELF USING CASE STUDIES

How to write your case study

As a professional or business owner, having a case study of successes can be an invaluable asset. Case studies provide clear evidence of your experience and skills and demonstrate that you can solve problems efficiently and achieve desired results. Whether you're looking to attract new clients, increase your reputation within the industry, or create meaningful connections with potential partners, investing time in producing and promoting your case study could be worthwhile. Check out some of the case studies on jaymandel.com.

The first step to creating a successful case study is to carefully consider what needs to be included in it.

1 *Identify the key points of the case*: What challenges did you solve? Which goals were achieved? What did you learn from this project? Defining the objectives before writing will give structure and guidance throughout the process.

2 *Choose the most appropriate medium for presenting your case*: Depending on the project and scope, you may want to consider different formats for setting out your stories such as a video presentation, infographics, or theatrical storytelling.

3 *Make sure your material is comprehensive*: Include details about stakeholder involvement and communication, timelines for each stage of completion, validation from experts in their field, and any analysis relating to how challenges were solved or goals were achieved.

4 *Have clearly defined outcome measurements*: It's crucial to have specific data around achievements to help foster tangible buy-in from partners in business or other clients who're considering working with you on future projects.

5 *Make use of visual aids*: Visual aids such as graphs and charts will help make complex ideas easier to understand while also improving aesthetics when sharing content online through social media channels such as LinkedIn or Twitter.

6 *Promote your case study*: Writing an excellent case study is just half of the job; it also needs effective promotion to generate greater visibility among potential stakeholders, which will consequently increase opportunities in the future. Promoting it on LinkedIn is usually a safe bet, given its concentrated audience. Still, there are other options available too, including:

   o Sharing via email campaigns: As long as messaging is not overly corporate, emails can be powerful when generating interest in prospective leads by highlighting past successes quickly and concisely.

   o Social media: When used correctly, social media channels are great for boosting awareness among your audiences if influencer participation can be organized around content-sharing protocols.

   o Blogging/commenting on forums and discussion boards: Writing guest blog posts is an excellent method for generating engagement amongst like-minded professionals.

   o Q&A sessions: Live sessions on popular forums allow anyone working elsewhere in the digital marketing space to gain recognition by offering advice using insights they may have acquired during previous work experiences. Try the Ask Me Anything feature on Reddit.

Your belief statement, your promise, and your potential

When crafting a belief statement, finding ways to differentiate yourself from competitors is essential. Try to identify the unique benefits of the brand you represent and the product you're marketing and construct a narrative that you can use across all consumer touchpoints. Customers will determine whether they should choose your company or a competitor's. Try using personalized language to express specifics about the product or service without being too generic. If there is nothing seemingly unique about your product, you would know this by now. However, you can influence how you position your product, deliver it, and engage with customers. If you don't believe you can make an impact, try, and see what happens! You may surprise yourself.

When writing an effective belief statement, keep the wording simple. You aren't doing yourself any favors by using overly fancy language. Be bold and outspoken. Explain why individuals need to choose the brand you represent over other companies offering similar products/services. Keep these statements clear and concise to avoid overloading customers with too much information. This will encourage them to read through your materials in total.

If you're looking to make a strong and memorable belief statement, look no further than the words of Seth Godin, who has provided an outline for making your own. We reviewed Seth Godin's simple marketing promise in chapter 4. Now it's time to do the same process for your brand. Rather than relying on try-hard catchphrases and gimmicks, focus on connecting what's important to you with what is important to others and tailor it to your audience.

Completing Seth Godin's three-sentence statement lets customers quickly identify if your product fits their values and needs. An effective mission statement should include three main components: belief, want, (and) get.[8] Furthermore, involving customers' values when crafting your message shows them they matter to the company and builds an emotional connection between them and your service/product.

Your product or service is what you offer to the world. It's the impression you make at work, home, and with friends. It's your secret power;

it's what makes you you. Identifying your intention for selling a product or service goes beyond an economic transaction. When contemplating why you intend to sell something, focus on how it will benefit others before considering the money you could make from the sale.

Here's how to craft a compelling three-sentence marketing promise that follows this advice.

My product is for people who believe...—Having a deep understanding of your audience is the key to effective marketing. It's not just about promoting yourself and your product, it's about understanding what they believe and desire before they meet you. Knowing their beliefs gives you the ability to craft persuasive messages tailored to them, helping shape their behavior regarding purchasing your product. With this approach, customers are more likely to buy from you because they already relate to the message you are providing versus an advertisement that could be seen as generic or untargeted. By keeping our focus on the audience and delivering meaningful messages that resonate with them, we dramatically increase the chances of success.

I will focus on people who want...—Customers are seeking companies that earnestly uphold their core values, and if you can attest to that through your logo and messaging, you will win their allegiance. This second sentence of your promise establishes robust ties between your organization's ideals and what your audience is looking for. When you nail this, it will make you feel like your company is the perfect convergence between what you believe in and what the consumer wants.

I promise that engaging with what I make will help you get it...—In conclusion, by addressing the gap between what customers want and what businesses deliver, we have created more than just a physical product or service; we have created an emotional connection. In doing so, we not only meet customer needs but exceed them and make the experience of buying from us genuinely transformative. We want our customers to feel empowered, inspired, and satisfied. Therefore, we focus on creating a feeling rather than just providing facts.

When attempting to project an emotion onto another person, it's essential to understand the difference between making someone feel something and feeling it yourself. A false promise of fulfilling an emotion can backfire—if you can't truly deliver on your pronouncement, then such a strategy will come undone eventually. When communicating with others or trying to manage expectations within personal relationships or professional settings, it pays dividends to remain honest about one's intentions from the start.

The difference between making someone feel and feeling something can be substantial in terms of relationships, business dealings, and more. Promises are often made to try and manipulate perceptions or emotions, but invoking false promises usually results in unintended consequences. If you have promised something that cannot truly be delivered, it's best to take a step back and analyze the situation. Collaborating with others is a great way to reach the desired result while being honest at the same time. Understanding how conditions may change over time helps you adjust your approach to get the most out of any situation.

When it comes to motivation and inspiration, one essential takeaway from my past experiences is that people shouldn't be afraid to sell themselves; if they think what they are offering can mean a lot to somebody else, then they are doing it right. Whether they deem their product as a small interruption or an actual lifeboat, everyone has something unique within themselves that can be of use to someone else.

The facets of your brand movement

A strong brand is more than just products or services; it requires a deep understanding of how customers view your company. As such, companies and brands need to create meaningful relationships with customers, looking out for their satisfaction along the way. Otherwise, they put themselves at risk of becoming irrelevant in the eyes of customers.

There are times when companies take a shortcut and forget the details, such as ignoring customers' feedback. When this happens, customers tend to feel unheard and overlooked. Unfortunately, this lack of attention can take its toll on a brand since the average customer wants to feel heard. In such instances, a request might be met with hollow words rather than action. These customers may act on the disconnect they're feeling with a brand and abandon them for a competing brand that takes better care of them.

Brand movement is the process of creating a powerful and recognizable brand that resonates with customers. It requires careful consideration of four aspects—product, community, utility, and simplicity—to create a powerful impact that will boost visibility and sustainability. By implementing all these steps in a cohesive fashion, companies can generate an effective brand strategy that will deliver successful results for their business.

Product: It all starts with the product or service you are offering to meet the demand of your audience. While creating a great product is essential, its success depends on how the brand is perceived in the market and how well it resonates with potential customers. Therefore, an organization's product is often its most powerful marketing tool as it reinforces customer trust in the brand itself.

Lifestyle: Creating customer loyalty isn't just about selling quality products; brands must also be associated with lifestyles their audiences aspire to live by positioning themselves as status symbols that evoke positive emotions. For example, luxury carmakers aren't only about selling cars; they present themselves as the epitome of speed, wealth, and ambition that discerning customers strive for when buying their vehicles.

Community: Coming up with an engaging story behind your product and tying it into modern culture can help you build strong communities around your brand and attract lots of long-time fans who will spread your brand message for you organically on social media platforms like Facebook and Twitter. Additionally, leveraging influencers such as celebrities or social media personalities to vouch for your brand can further amplify word-of-mouth referrals from existing customers resulting in more purchases in the future.

Utility: Offering useful information or services that enable customers to gain skills and competency is an important way of both connecting with them emotionally and also providing them with long-lasting value. By equipping customers with a sense of achievement related to their engagement with the product or service, they become more likely to remain loyal customers even when new competition emerges. It's a powerful marketing technique that can set your company apart from its rivals in the long run.

Simplicity: Too much complexity can scare away customers, even if the new product or service is revolutionary. People prefer products and services that are easy to use and don't require long instructions or difficult steps. If customers must read dozens of pages before using a new product, they may be put off and instead rely on familiar products that are easier to use, as it requires less effort for them in the short term. Long instructions can also be very intimidating for some people and may cause them to avoid taking risks with something new. In this sense, complexity can hinder the adoption of new offerings no matter how innovative they might be. After you, as a team, agree on what you are trying to convey, make sure that you edit, edit, edit. Cut every word and idea that doesn't add value to your point of view.

Connect with customers with the nesting doll

Do you need help bridging the gap with consumers? It can be challenging for businesses and customers to connect, especially when one needs help understanding the other's needs. But understanding, addressing, and satisfying these needs is the key to business success. With a creative, holistic approach, the nesting doll, created by professional strategy teacher Julian Cole, helps businesses to more effectively understand and address customers' wants and needs. This innovative strategy gives you an effective system, from identifying the problem to offering a solution to achieving goals that benefit both the company and the consumer.

The nesting doll provides an effective way for companies to communicate with their customer base, as it speaks directly to them clearly and precisely. By utilizing this strategy, companies can break through all the other noise and clearly state their message, ensuring that the customers receive the information they need. When I first saw the nesting doll, I knew instantly that it would make a great addition to my lecture material as its messaging would help complete the marketing mix puzzle.

Each stage of the nesting doll focuses on identifying consumer needs creatively while allowing businesses to meet these needs without sacrificing long-term profitability. It ultimately aims to provide solutions that nurture customer relationships towards higher engagement and strong loyalty. The concept seeks to ensure that a company's marketing efforts are focused on the customer, not just what the company wants. This means starting at the beginning and identifying the goal. For example, is the company looking to raise awareness, generate leads, or increase sales? Understanding this will allow companies to identify where they should focus their efforts—such as which channels and platforms they should use to reach potential customers—to see an impact in those areas. It helps companies move away from general approaches and apply specific tactics that get them closer to their end goal.

Moving to the customer's problem. Rather than simply offering solutions that do not match what the consumer wants, take time to really listen and engage with them to identify underlying motivations and frustrations within the context of their experience of buying or using your product or service. Investigate every angle by digging deeper into customer trends, preferences, interests, values, spending habits, etc.

Next, how can the company and customer, and everyone, win? With a solution that meets their needs with one holistic approach rather than several isolated ones such as separate channels or methods. This step demands creativity from businesses because it requires understanding all possible solutions for any given problem instead of just one single answer for all cases.

Finally, set achievable goals with your business so you can easily measure progress while maintaining alignment between objectives and desired outcomes. Setting clear benchmarks makes it easier to track whether a campaign was successful or not much later down the road—especially when considering ROI in terms of both top-line sales figures as well as bottom-line profits, which may often vary depending on factors like industry-specific dynamics or even current market sentiment at any given moment in time!

In summary, the nesting methodology forces the marketer to understand and analyze the problem from all angles and eliminates fuzzy logic and tone-deaf campaigns. Your business problems should be rooted in what you are trying to solve, which is only very interesting to you. Consumers care about what they want and how they can get it. They don't care why you like it or what you think it should be. Their interest is in solving their problems. So, if you want to know what people want, watch them. What they say is what they want. You can learn everything else from what they buy.

This is the nesting doll template:

- **BRAND NAME** (business problem)
- **PROBLEM IS** (consumer + problem)
- **HOWEVER** (insight)
- **WE NEED TO** (solution)
- **SO THAT** (consumer goal)
- **HELPING TO** (business goal)

Let's examine this step by step, for example for germ-killing disinfectants:

- **PROBLEM IS** mothers see germ-kill as overkill
- **HOWEVER,** many mothers feel that protection is an instinctive act of love
- **WE NEED TO** make the strength of company X product's protection as every day as strong as the strength of a mother's protection
- **SO THAT** moms feel assured they're doing the most to protect their kids
- **HELPING TO** increase usage of products by 20%

As a business, it's essential to have an effective marketing strategy that resonates with your customers. This means understanding their needs and creating solutions that solve those problems in a way that is both perceived as valuable by the customer and profitable for the business. An example of this in action can be seen through company X's marketing efforts to increase the usage of their germ-killing disinfectants by 20 percent. Let's look at how the nesting of customer needs was used to create this successful campaign.

1 Identify the problem: The first step in building an effective strategy is identifying the problem that the company needs to solve. In company X's case, the problem was that mothers viewed germ-kill as overkill and had less usage than desired of its product.

2 Understand your audience: It's important to understand your audience and what motivates them so you can build messaging around those motivators. In this case, company X discovered that many mothers felt protection was an instinctive act of love.

3 Create a solution: Armed with this insight, company X set out to make their strength of protection every day as strong as the strength of a mother's protection—ensuring moms are doing all they need to protect their children.

4 Craft your messaging and platforms: Once a solution has been crafted, it's time to choose which channels to promote it the most effectively. In this example, company X used traditional TV spots combined with print ads and social media outreach on relevant parenting accounts to reach its audience where they could be influenced most strongly.

5 Measure success: Finally, once your campaigns have launched, it's essential to measure how successful they are at solving your goal— increasing usage by 20 percent. Utilizing metrics such as sales figures or website visits can help determine if you've achieved your objective and give you data for further tweaking should improvements still need to be made.

Who is your audience?

Everyone wants their message to travel far and wide and to be heard by the right people who will appreciate and purchase the products or services. To do this, we need to know who your audience is and what motivates them to act. The nesting doll technique and the simple marketing promise can help any business better understand its demographic and what will make them tick. Once these methods are completed, business owners can focus on their specific audiences.

Defining a particular audience in branding is essential because it provides insight into the market and what they may be looking for. It allows you to craft messaging, offers, visuals, and product specifics that interest your potential customer. This helps businesses create effective content marketing initiatives and ensure efficient use of marketing budgets by narrowing down spending areas.

Market segmentation is essential to breaking your audience into distinct groups based on specific criteria. This allows marketers to identify customer needs, wants, and preferences. These are the criteria we established earlier, your intention, which is connected to your values and your company's values, which, if done correctly, will also relate to your customer's values and wants and needs of the story they tell themselves about themselves.

The market segmentation section should come after creating your marketing promise or brand statement. After you have applied the nesting doll strategy, the goal is to see glimmers of segmentation in those two exercises and then take these ideas and build upon them with the official segmentation exercise.

The steps in conducting market segmentation include the following:

1 Identify the criteria for the segmentation (e.g. geographical location, demographics, lifestyle).

2 Organize the data according to these criteria using analytical methods such as cluster analysis or other statistical techniques. See chapter 8 on market research for more details.

3 Evaluate and assess the segments for their potential profitability.

4 Develop and test value propositions for each of the segments identified.

Personas convey how audience segments interact with your brand

Personas are a great way for brand managers to understand their customer base and ensure that their marketing campaigns capture their target audience. Personas provide insights into the likes and dislikes of customers, allowing marketers to tailor their messaging, visuals, and keywords to get the most out of a campaign.

Identifying characteristics

By analyzing the data from existing consumers' surveys/interviews, you should be able to come away with broad characteristics that can be divided across different consumer types (e.g. Millennial vs. Baby Boomer). Use these trends among specific consumer types combined with other factors like demographics to create three to five different personas that mirror real people within each segment of your target audience—this includes giving each persona distinct names too!

Building these personas involves coming up with general demographic groups like gender, age range, and interests and then developing more detailed information such as job titles, income level, hobbies, and backgrounds. However, some companies find it difficult to create visual representations for each persona due lack of resources. Here are some steps you can take to help you overcome this obstacle:

Start by defining the basic characteristics of each persona—for example, gender and ethnicity. This helps position the avatar to become memorable within a particular subcategory of your customers.

Once you have determined their characteristics and job role, select appropriate clothing pieces and accessories that fit their personality and role perfectly. Depending on your audience, this could include anything from casual streetwear-inspired apparel to smart office wear.

Utilizing celebrities or cartoon versions of characters could also help reinforce certain messages while simultaneously creating fun visuals surrounding them. Furthermore, making sure all decorative elements used throughout the avatar's look (hairstyle, jewelry choice, props) reflect the desired emotions developed during the persona definition stage is important when it comes to building iconic figureheads in digital marketing campaigns or visual stories around products/services offered by a company.

As times change, so do customer needs, so be sure to revisit customer personas at least once a year—more often if there have been changes in the marketplace or an increased focus on specific sectors of potential customers. Updating personas is essential to leading any marketing team in the desired direction while ensuring your message resonates gently and securely with prospective clients.

Jobs-to-be-done framework

A jobs-to-be-done (JTBD) framework has become popular among marketers and product designers over the past few years, providing an easy way to understand your customer's needs.[9] This framework is based on the core principle that customers hire products, services, or experiences for "jobs" or tasks they want to achieve. While this job may be enjoyable or desirable, jobs to be done are ultimately driven by the result that consumers seek—which could vary from a concrete outcome (e.g. purchase of a product) to an emotional response (feeling accomplished). Knowing how and why consumers use a particular product helps inform messaging, design, and development decisions. The overall objective of personas is to help build better buyer profiles, while JTBD frameworks aim to identify human needs before diving into problem-solving.

JTBD frameworks are different from personas in many ways. While personas take marketers through customers' activities, inclinations, longings, and drives, a JTBD framework assists you in comprehending the motivations behind customer behavior.

Personas tend to focus on broad characteristics of personality types such as age range, gender, etc. In contrast, JTBD frameworks focus on understanding user motivations in terms of outcomes instead of targets, e.g. "I need a smartphone that will allow me to check emails quickly."

In addition to introducing the customer problem, it is important to focus on why it matters and how your product or service can provide a resolution. It needs to be persuasive and leave customers wanting more, ensuring they understand the importance of finding a solution through your company rather than another competitor.

Personas are typically built with qualitative data such as survey responses, focus group interviews, and ethnographic research. In contrast, JTBD frameworks look at quantitative data from analytics tools and customer feedback forms which help identify patterns across buying behavior within different consumer segments for improved decision-making.

Personas rely mainly on demographic variables such as age, gender, marital status, location, and income to create an archetype of the customer. This helps marketers develop messages that should resonate with a particular segment. On the other hand, a JTBD framework relies on behavioral analytics to explore what customers are trying to achieve when using a product or service. By looking at user activity logs, companies can attempt to figure out how people use their products and what it is they're trying to accomplish. This information can be used to tailor the messaging and better focus marketing efforts— to only on those customers who are likely interested in the product's end goal(s).

Persona creation produces output such as expectations maps and touchpoints. In contrast, JTBD frameworks result in pivot questions and prototypes that assist businesses in validating newly crafted solutions more efficiently with customers than relying exclusively on market research techniques alone.

Don't create followers. Be in it with your customers

In product development, an "end user" is a person who interacts with a particular product or uses the product's output. Since marketing differs from product development, why is the word used so often in marketing and customer conversations?

Who wants to be called a user?

Everyone who purchases something, i.e. all of us, is a customer when you categorize them as such. However, in today's world, where businesses primarily interact with customers digitally, keeping an interpersonal and human connection to your customers is one of the most crucial elements of having success.

As a business, calling your customers "end users" rather than creating a more personal connection can make it seem like they are not crucial to your business. In such a robotic and automated world, forming a human relationship with them will help your brand remain engaging and up to date.

It all comes down to how you communicate verbally and non-verbally with your customers. The words you choose are very significant in how others see you and how you perceive the world.

Establishing a connection with customers is critical before any interactions. You can't be close to somebody you don't yet know, so getting to grips with their likes and dislikes, preferences, and persona would help build a relationship.

Innovative companies give customers a feeling of value to remain loyal. Here are some easy ways to begin:

- Ensure personalized messages are used for your clients; an individual who perceives the feelings of being treasured will stay with you.[10]

- To leave a lasting impression on your customers, customize your landing pages to provide the optimal experience. Implementing a strategy and using the right tools can help you tailor your content, design, and customer experience to meet your customers' needs.

- Use chat functionality to get to know customers and connect with them based on their needs. Focus more on customer service, support, and satisfaction than community management and social selling.

- It may seem counterintuitive, but negative customer feedback is one of the best gifts your business can receive. Establishing communication with customers, getting their input, and understanding even a bad experience will help improve in the future.

A brand that wants authentic engagement should focus on leading and engaging with, not just amassing, followers. Your brand needs to promise something to someone specific, and if someone chooses to engage, they should not be called a follower. Why? Because a follower is someone who doesn't think for themselves and blindly follows the leader without question. A leader, on the other hand, inspires others to follow them because they stand for something specific and are authentic in their message. When you focus on leading, you create a community of engaged individuals who believe in what you stand for and are willing to spread the word about your brand. So, ditch the term followers and focus on leading instead. Those who engage with you will follow suit, despite what you call them.

When the content marketing revolution started, it was an eye-opening experience. Brands went from talking about themselves and navel-gazing to creating content machines. They created and flooded the internet with any content that could remotely relate to what they do and how they do it. In many ways, this can be good for long-tail searches. A long-tail search is when people search for something specific, and your content addresses their wants and needs. Several companies do this content well.

Stories need structure to have maximum impact

Developing a story-driven framework is a great way to harness the power of storytelling and maximize its impact. By reviving powerful moments into stories, we can create an emotionally charged narrative that will bring people together and give them something to believe in. Not only is this great for marketing, it also gives us a platform to share our experiences with others and make a positive impact. Through this framework, we can craft inspiring stories that bring out the best in ourselves and those around us.

Your company's culture is the foundation upon which everything else is built. Without a strong shared sense of ideals, purpose, and values, any attempts to create a movement within the organization may fail. It's essential to understand what makes your organization unique so that you can focus on building it into your culture—developing its identity and setting yourself apart from the competition.

Choose an emotional hook

A key component of any successful story is emotion, particularly regarding movements. Choose an emotional hook that resonates with your audience, so they feel compelled to act by sharing your message or becoming more actively involved in the cause behind the movement.

Outline your story

Now that you've identified who will be consuming this content and what will motivate them, it's time to create a blueprint for how this story will play out and come together. Developing a beginning, middle, and end helps keep everyone focused on the same goal: getting from point A (the impetus for creating this story) to point B (the exciting conclusion).

Stories are conversation starters that offer insight into you as an individual, what you value, and your perception of the world. As social and emotional beings, our reality is intertwined with others, making our stories worth sharing. Our experiences might be unique, but their reoccurrence makes them relatable. Stories help you connect with your audience while evoking their sense of belongingness, allowing storytellers to become personally invested in their clients' stories and lives.

The structural flow of a story must address certain elements. My job is to help my clients connect with the value of their journey and translate it into a powerful, meaningful, and moving narration. I hold sessions with my clients to discuss their ideas and opinions as we develop their brands. Over the years, I noticed a pattern emerge, which allowed me to build my own proprietary marketing storytelling methodology.

Introducing a new way to think about your story.[11]

THE PAST—HOW IT'S BEEN

Your journey is unique to you. It has challenged you to highlight a weakness or shortcoming you see in yourself, your community, or society at large. This is the kind of thing that you see from your vantage point and can't unsee. When you see it, you know what you are witnessing relates and connects with other people, and you can't wait to share it with the world!

THE PRESENT—HOW WE SEE IT

It would be best if you had a perspective that enlightens others. It could have been difficult, tiring, or frustrating. Or it was enlightening, joyful, and crazy. But it must be novel and relatable to be meaningful and drive impact. You have a point of view on why and how your experience must immediately address this problem, which you MUST spell out in writing.

THE FUTURE—HOW WE'LL CHANGE IT TOGETHER

Your resolution to conquer the uncovered issue needs immediate attention but will only be solved with others. Seeing you invested in guiding your story empowers your readers to join your movement. Your story must give people hope. Your audience wishes to see you involved in their stories to create a united force against a common problem. How do you plan to turn the situation in your favor? How can others benefit from it? Time to get people to join you in your movement.

Bringing your story to life

Story-doing is a powerful tool for creating meaningful connections with your audience.[12] It's about taking storytelling to the next level by allowing customers to engage with your story in a whole new way. Before you can begin using story-doing, you will need to develop a captivating storyline that relates to the brand narrative you built in the previous chapter based on audience personas and your brand's "identity" and "intention."

Start by outlining the beginning, middle, and end of your story. Think carefully about how you want to introduce the characters and what the conflict resolution should be at the end of your tale.

For customers to connect with your story, it's important that they can relate to characters in the narrative. When developing characters for your storyline, think about things like their goals, values, and dreams—all qualities that make them human and more relatable for viewers.

Interactive flows allow customers to make choices as they experience narrative story-doing. This makes the experience much more engaging and rewarding, which increases engagement and encourages customers to stay with the product or brand for longer. It also helps marketers identify trends in the market, offering creative solutions tailored towards a particular brand's objectives. Furthermore, calls to action within such interactive flow paths can be incredibly beneficial if done appropriately and according to brand prospects. Predictive analytics derived from various data resources can also help evaluate different stages of an interactive flow over varying times, helping project teams to better assess progress and results.

Develop multiple touchpoints

Your story should be developed across multiple touchpoints. After all, stories don't just exist in one format or medium, so decide which platforms are best suited for the brand or product story, such as social media posts, blog posts, videos, etc., then create specific types of content designed around those kinds of touchpoints. This allows you to cultivate deeper engagement with your audience by cueing into each platform's strengths—videos work particularly well on Instagram while longer blog posts offer more detail on websites—essentially allowing viewers/readers/listeners different ways of consuming the same core concepts while still getting something unique out of each piece they view/read/listen to.

A good story is heard, but a great story is lived. So how do you want people to receive yours?

Stories are conversation starters that offer insight into you as an individual, what you value, and your perception of the world. As social and emotional beings, our reality is intertwined with others, making our stories worth sharing. Our experiences might be unique, but their reoccurrence makes them relatable. Stories help you connect with your audience while evoking their sense of belonging, allowing storytellers to become personally invested in their clients' stories and lives.

Anchor core values in storytelling

Successful movements tend to thrive on this idea of storytelling; connecting core values with compelling stories helps people get excited about participating in the movement inside and outside the office walls. To build something special, remind everyone why their contributions matter by linking work goals with larger narrative arcs—tell stories that help individuals feel valued for their efforts rather than just letting them know how much work needs to be done.

Prompts

We live in the age of "niche." It used to be a novelty to have a dating site. Tinder and match.com stood for "dating." You could sort by the type of person you were looking for. But over time, the internet had other ideas. There are now specialized sites for older people, younger people, Jewish people, Christian people, single parents, and Muslims—it doesn't matter, but what does matter is that people want to connect with something before they engage with your product. And by talking to a particular audience and building a product that addresses their specific wants and needs, you can facilitate that connection your audience wants to make with the world around them. It is no use being able to sort a generic website for race, religion, or a particular type of person you are looking for if that website doesn't attract a critical mass of people who fit that criterion. And if the operations of this company do not treat certain audience members with white gloves, showing them that they understand them and add value to their lives, then why they would join?

Can you look at your brand in a way that mirrors what I just described in online dating? You bet! (And, if you couldn't, I wouldn't have mentioned it.) If you have one website for your brand, and from that website, people can come to different audiences, why not experiment, and see if you can modify your brand to meet your audience better where they are? This goes beyond creating a technical way to sort by a particular audience. Here is a fundamental shift to how you look at serving specific niches in your audience, so they feel like they are the most critical person in the world. You will not attract an audience if you don't make them feel special. When teams are built around addressing their needs, putting something into the marketplace will always lead to a customer.

Personalization—are you talking to me?

Are you looking for ways to make your brand stand out from the competition? If so, you may have considered personalizing your product or service to reach a specific audience. Personalization is so much more than just knowing someone's name and demographics. To truly engage customers in this new era of marketing, businesses must understand their customers on a deeper level and deliver personalized experiences that are both impactful and memorable. Here's what you need to know about personalization today.

Pursue multiple channels: With many communication channels available, deciding which formats best suit audiences can take time. Utilize email, chatbots, and voice-enabled interactions like Alexa and Google Assistant to capture more leads for special interest-related categories, industry trends, or deals per audience segment.

Use niche-focused landing pages: Having individualized webpages for each niche will help you cater better to this hyper-specific crowd since it allows website visitors to quickly find information about pages tailored specifically for them without having to navigate through all the other sections of your retail site. Selecting geographical areas on the homepage feature settings that appear on mobile devices via GPS coordinates or providing personalized content, such as blog posts or videos dedicated towards each niche from experts who are involved in those specific topics, offers viewers assurance that they are dealing with professionals who know precisely what they need when it comes to finding solutions for their situations at hand.

Track results through analytics: Systems like Google Analytics allow you to track page visits by demographic attributes such as language and gender (or other personally identifiable characteristics). This will give you a better idea of how well certain landing pages perform among different niche audiences, which could potentially reveal additional opportunities which could be further pursued in future campaigns or initiatives. Furthermore, monitoring your user activity metrics via analytics can help point out technical issues on desktop or mobile versions of the site, which might go undiscovered otherwise.

Show off authentic and engaging brand personality: Always keep up with trends within industries concerning topics related to brand/ customer relationships so you're seen as a knowledgeable resource relative to each individual topic rather than just another salesperson striving for buyers when necessary. At its core, on-trend conversations should always include showing off a genuine personality instead of portraying yourself as "all business." Creating specialized content along these lines adds human interest while still emphasizing specific points interested customers may want to address ahead of moving onto other matters, positively improving conversions over time amidst desirable niches overall. Add value and solve real problems or even solve a problem that customers didn't know existed.

Do you need to remember to do essential tasks or feel overwhelmed by your daily responsibilities? If so, you're not alone. It's easy to get overwhelmed with the demands of everyday life, and many of us need a little reminder to help manage our activities and stay on track. And many companies offer us reminders not just because they make our lives easier but because it is an excellent way to add value and create a meaningful and memorable experience.

In a world of technology and automation, many companies have incorporated reminders into their customer service which can be both timely and add value to their customers' lives. Reminders provide an added level of convenience and create meaningful experiences for customers—not just from a functional standpoint but from an emotional one. Customers appreciate being reminded of things like appointments or due dates, as it relieves them of some of the responsibilities that often come with modern life. In turn, this can lead to a greater sense of loyalty towards the company providing the reminder service.

In the age of e-commerce, Prime Day has become one of the leading shopping holidays, allowing shoppers to find deals on various items from Amazon and other online retailers. But what is Prime Day? How was it invented, and why has it become so popular? Here's a look at what Prime Day is and how it came to be.

Prime Day was first introduced in 2015 by Amazon to celebrate its 20th anniversary.[13] It was initially established primarily as a way for Amazon Prime members—those who had signed up for the annual subscription service—to get special discounts and offers on products they might not otherwise have access to.

Since then, other retailers, both inside the United States and out, have been getting in on the trend of offering company-specific sales and promotions. This goes beyond "holiday sales" during bank holidays and federal holidays. Brand-specific dates can happen throughout the year.

Today, companies like Walmart, Target, and eBay have brand-specific holiday-style promotions. These one-day sales typically offer discounts for shoppers looking for specific items or huge savings opportunities.

Cyber Monday is another increasingly popular shopping holiday related to Black Friday, where customers can snatch up bargains online instead of waiting until stores open on Thanksgiving weekend.

With so many options out there, consumers can now find deals throughout the year, not just during traditional brick-and-mortar holiday seasons such as Christmas or Black Friday.

Buyer prompts like these are powerful tools for motivating people to act. Whether in public, within the workplace, or behind the scenes, prompting people to do something—visiting a place, submitting a photo related to your travels, or other activities—can be incredibly effective in leading individuals in a more positive direction.

Google is one of the most renowned companies for leveraging this prompting technique. Google effectively implements prompts into its products by incentivizing users with rewards and recognition for their work. For example, customers are often sent notifications with suggestions about submitting photos from places they have recently visited. Upon doing so, users receive rewards for following through on Google's suggestion; this makes it easy for them to act on their requests. Moreover, allowing customers to see how many people have viewed their work plays into our natural urge for validation from others. Through these prompts, Google ensures we are providing them with their needed information while taking care of our interests.

Another advantage of reminders for both parties is that it eliminates miscommunication between them. In an age where technology makes communication rapid and efficient, reminders can help prevent misunderstandings that could occur due to poor communication techniques or inattention to detail. They also contribute positively to customer relationships by reducing confusion regarding establishing when events occur and who is responsible for tasks.

Finally, reminders like these are essential when customers who track progress want updates on progress or results they inquired about previously—a feature no longer out of reach with new technologies like SMS texting notifications and email alerts in place today. Offering periodic updates, especially if they require minimal effort on the part of the team to inform them, is a great way not only to remind them but show how much you value their relationship with your business, further building loyalty between the parties involved even if those efforts cost very little in terms of time or money expended upfront.

In conclusion, many companies offer us reminders because they make our lives easier and are an excellent way to add value and create meaningful and memorable experiences. Implementing timely reminder services guarantees trustworthiness between businesses and customers while helping increase organizational efficiency by enhancing communication channels throughout entire processes from beginning to end.

Creating a successful movement within an organization requires careful planning and consideration of multiple channels for involvement. It needs to be communicated outwardly through social media, have an engaging website as its home base, contain elements that allow for interactive contributions from visitors, and involve real-world activities to further increase awareness of the cause.

Achieving this involves much more than just funneling employee engagement through one channel. To spark dialogue, generate participation from all departments throughout the business, and ensure that no one is left out when decisions are made or feedback is given, organizations should use multiple efforts to create a movement that successfully engages their employees. Here's how!

Provide multiple channels for involvement: For a movement within an organization to truly take off, more than just funneling all employee engagement through one channel will be required. Instead, creating multiple channels for involvement allows for more widespread participation throughout all departments in your business. It helps ensure that no one gets left out when making decisions or giving feedback. Consider ways everyone can contribute—whether through conversations with colleagues or formal brainstorming sessions—and consider providing incentives if feasible.

Spread your message far and wide: One way to amplify your message outwardly is through social media; post daily updates using hashtags related to your campaign and encourage active employees on social media platforms such as Twitter or LinkedIn to share these posts often with their followers. This helps spread awareness of what's happening inside your company but also creates opportunities for external audiences—potential customers or industry professionals—to learn more about your organization's initiatives.

Create an engaging website: Having a website as the home base for your campaign is essential. It should include information about why the campaign exists, how people can get involved, success stories from those who have participated, and blog posts about the latest developments or news related to your cause. In addition, try to make sure that the website is interactive—invite feedback from visitors and allow them to share their stories with others through comment sections, forums, or polls.

Get out on social media: Social media is one of the best ways to spread awareness of your movement and reach potential advocates quickly. Facebook, Twitter, and Instagram are particularly effective channels for this purpose, allowing you to quickly build up a following of people interested in participating in your cause. Try to use visual elements such as images or videos wherever possible when sharing content on social media—studies show these often receive higher engagement rates than plain text posts.

Organize events: Online engagement is excellent for spreading awareness about your cause, but real-world activities have much more power to mobilize supporters into taking tangible action towards effecting change within their communities (which is probably one of the main goals of any social movement). In addition, organizing events/actions such as protests or fundraisers around key dates related to the issue helps rally groups who may feel inspired by similar values or beliefs—leading to more active levels of participation among supporters, which can result in a more significant impact off-screen too.

Measure effectiveness: Although storytelling is traditionally thought of as an art form rather than backed by science and data metrics, knowing whether specific pieces of content generate better results than others can help inform future decision-making processes as well as assessing whether the original goal was achieved through those efforts. Be sure to measure performance metrics such as engagement rates across all platforms whenever possible to keep track of successes; this helps guide future project planning and failures that can inform improvement strategies in the future.

White space and recommendations

White or negative space is a design area that does not contain any text or visual elements. Identifying and utilizing white space in a branding project is essential because it creates a sense of balance and clarity by allowing individual elements to stand out and be more noticeable. This can help to emphasize important details, making it easier for the audience to digest content. Additionally, white space helps to make designs look more organized and professional. And while the white space I mentioned above is critical, this differs from the white space I am talking about.

The white space we are speaking of here is the market opportunities left undiscovered by competitors. By studying existing segments, buyer personas, and trend reports and combining this knowledge with quantitative data such as market size and opportunity metrics, as well as qualitative intel like customer feedback and recent events, you should be able to gain insight into a potential white space that will give you an edge over your competition.

Once you've identified potential opportunities from those filters, break them down into core themes that summarize their purpose and align with the products/services of your brand. Keep these themes rooted in data and insightful enough for creative inspiration during the testing phase. Consider using this exercise with multiple departments to ensure that every voice is included when developing ideas.

Using those core themes as a guide, develop strategies for showing and representing them within your brand narrative: tone of voice, key messages, storytelling techniques, etc. Iterate them based on internal feedback or external factors until they meet the company values while staying true to the actual needs of customers outside the market conditions already present when these themes were defined (i.e. potential new trends). Next, map and test plan. This is where timelines come into play, articulating how long each idea will take to be brought to life (for example, digital campaigns, focus groups, etc). Keep track of milestones or checklists along its roadmap to measure effectiveness—allowing you to justify business models accordingly.

Developing a viable product solution requires integrating customer insights and establishing the right tactics. It is then necessary to hypothesize if the idea has commercial viability. Next, analyze and utilize various data sources such as surveys, metrics, figures, statistics, and observations/reflections from customer feedback. These data points should inform the next steps in product development, such as launch date, channels used for promotion, etc. Ultimately, armed with relevant data points, it becomes easier to establish a timeline for product implementation and potentially go-to-market strategies.

Before any real action is taken, purpose-driven assumptions and ideas must be validated. If a good idea matures, it can then enter the branding process. This iterative process involves gathering user input and making necessary changes to ensure that the best possible portrayal of the product or service is available for those who need it. It should also possess the flexibility to stand out from competitors while providing something tailored for niche audiences. This will ensure that no matter what the market says, even if it's non-conforming, your brand will remain relevant over time.

Now is your time to make your mark

"So, what are you waiting for?" as my grandmother would say. Enough with all the strategy, it's time to focus on the third I: implementation. Your implementation, naturally, should bridge your identity with your intention, both as an individual and as a company.

Embracing the challenge of implementation can be a daunting task. Still, with the right strategy and approach, it is possible to create systems that bring together your identity, vision, and intention. Once these elements unite, you have created an executable plan to reach your desired goal. To get you started on the journey, in the next chapter, we will review how these approaches come together in regular daily life and form a systemized approach to reaching your objectives. Then, by understanding each element individually and creating a bridge between them, you can begin taking action to reach the success you are looking for.

Endnotes

1 Aldridge, K (2020, March 5) The origin story of Sweetgreen, how brands are born, howbrandsareborn.com/blog/sweetgreen (archived at https://perma.cc/4TMC-REF5)

2 Sweetgreen (nd) Our mission, sweetgreen.com/mission (archived at https://perma.cc/8GS7-98KM)

3 Burnett, L (2018, November 23) McDonald's: #ReindeerReady by Leo Burnett, The Drum, thedrum.com/creative-works/project/leo-burnett-mcdonalds-reindeerready (archived at https://perma.cc/B33A-2LVZ)

4 Binlot, A (2019, February 28) Nike and Serena Williams inspire women to "Dream Crazier" with new campaign, *Forbes*, forbes.com/sites/abinlot/2019/02/28/nike-and-serena-williams-inspire-women-to-dream-crazier-with-new-campaign/ (archived at https://perma.cc/PE85-2RMV)

5 Dove (2021, January 27) Dove Real Beauty Sketches, dove.com/us/en/stories/campaigns/real-beauty-sketches.html (archived at https://perma.cc/P3QC-A8Z8)

6 Wikipedia (2022, July 17) Dove Real Beauty Sketches, Wikimedia Foundation, en.wikipedia.org/wiki/Dove_Real_Beauty_Sketches (archived at https://perma.cc/U4CQ-7SF4)

7 Kaplan D A (2022, May 10) Absolut Vodka puts its brand behind struggling LGBTQ+ bars, Adweek, adweek.com/brand-marketing/absolut-vodka-puts-its-brand-behind-struggling-lgbtq-bars/ (archived at https://perma.cc/ZK7R-DZ52)

8 Godin, S (2019) *This is Marketing: You can't be seen until you learn to see*, Penguin Business

9 Ulwick, A W (2016) *Jobs to Be Done: Theory to Practice*, Idea Bite Press

10 Mandel, J (2019, April 15) Users are Losers!, LinkedIn Pulse, linkedin.com/pulse/users-losers-jay-mandel (archived at https://perma.cc/GQ8B-DZR6)

11 Mandel, J (2022, September 18) Introducing the past, present, future story roadmap, Your Brand Coach, jaymandel.com/introducing-the-past-present-future-story-roadmap/ (archived at https://perma.cc/79PW-CJXW)

12 Montague, T (2018, February 5) Good companies are storytellers. Great companies are storydoers, *Harvard Business Review*, hbr.org/2013/07/good-companies-are-storyteller (archived at https://perma.cc/J5P3-TKUS)

13 Malin, Z (2021, June 7) How Amazon Prime day has grown and changed since 2015, NBC News, nbcnews.com/select/shopping/amazon-prime-day-history-ncna1269819 (archived at https://perma.cc/9YP8-H7BS)

Conclusion

Executing Your Plan

At the beginning of this book, we delved into your "identity." To be an individual who achieves all their potential—with evolutions of how we think about work, technology, and marketplaces—there is ample opportunity to have your cake and eat it too.

We then shifted our focus to connecting your identity with clear objectives, utilizing your interests, skills, and enthusiasm to assist the company employing you—whether they be giants or organizations owned by yourself. This may involve employees in customer service roles smiling at customers, yet having nothing behind that smile, which will be noticeable.

You've identified yourself and your company, done the necessary research to build a trustworthy team, and have a particular scope of work listing what should be included and excluded, with a vision of success in mind. However, all that hard work will go to waste without seeing it through until the end, which is why it's essential to further our discussion of "implementation" in this last chapter.

It's the execution and, to be precise, the purposeful implementation—that is, the action taken to make a plan happen—that makes all the difference. It's where many brilliant ideas go to die, but with proper implementation, you can turn your brilliant idea into reality.

It's time to apply what you've now created throughout this book and put a stake in the ground which will put your firm ahead of the competition. This chapter contains various approaches to think about and templates to utilize for defining your strategy.

And then comes your movement, which acts as the icing on the top and enriches the customer experience. Your movement, presented as a promise, builds a deep connection with the audience. Just like identity, your personal or company's movement also needs to be registered and organized by yourself. You can only perceive your movement (or come up with one) by truly understanding who you are and how your values resonate with your customers.

Connecting your vision, plans, and actions with psychology helps you better understand your skills and plan of action. To understand what goes on around you, it is imperative to figure out what goes inside your head. And most often, we need to be aware of what we truly desire and are capable of!

When you understand who you are, what you do, and why you do it, you are well-positioned to lead change in your organization. It's time to put all the groundwork you've done into action and actualize your story. It's time for implementation.

We all have grand plans, dreams, and aspirations. But success will only come if you work hard to make those dreams come true. Using the techniques taught in this book, you can elevate the game and make real progress towards achieving your goals as a Meaningful Marketer (should I trademark that?).

To bridge the gap between your big dream and the on-ground implementation, I want to leave you with three golden nuggets that may form the foundation of your next big idea. Over the past five years, there have been multiple moments of realization for me, and with each of these moments, I get closer to being my authentic self. And more recently, it all came together for me; the eureka moment didn't come at any grand event or academic moment but while writing this book. The process of clarifying my approach for learners like you has reignited the flame of having a deeper purpose, and with that came the reinvention of myself.

Let's dive deeper into the three golden nuggets, and then I'll leave you to experience the magic for yourself!

#1 The eureka moment comes from unexpected places

At first, it can feel like you will never find a solution as you exhaust different theories and formulas with no luck. But then, something magical happens, and the pieces instantly fall into place. Suddenly everything makes sense, and your hard work is rewarded with a breakthrough in understanding. This eureka moment is gratifying and reminds us why exploring mathematics, science, and other disciplines can be so enjoyable.

When you come across something intriguing, such as a sign on the street or an energizing song, it sparks your curiosity and encourages you to delve deeper. As marketers, we need to think quickly, so we act fast and put it out there when this happens. Whether it's a quick TikTok you create while walking on Broadway or a note you take quickly to capture a precious moment of imagination, the world constantly provides new creative opportunities.

My TikTok series, The Mind of a Marketer, was created by looking at a sign on the street. I've always been curious about billboards, signs, and even small graffiti pieces, and exploring the world around me allows for unexpected eureka moments. My walks around NYC are now not just for running errands but a constant source of marketing innovation. Whether you're from NYC or Tokyo, you can also find little moments of inspiration.

It's essential to understand who you are, what your business stands for, who your audience is, and which elements should be included or excluded to provide an outstanding customer experience. All these components cohesively define what your street presence and beyond says about you as a business. Do you want to see the moment I came to this conclusion? Visit jaymandel.com.

#2 You can't get a comprehensive perspective from a narrow peer group

Back in 2017, I got connected with a few partners outside of the States.

We've all encountered such partnerships: the Indian software guy who magically codes something genius, the marketing guru from Singapore with a deep understanding of the Asian markets, the Korean project manager who speaks broken English but never misses a deadline, and the Chinese freelancer who only works at midnight but solves half of your worries—you get the idea.

And while many of these partnerships may have yet to work for you, the magic starts when it does. When you find a team that bridges the gap between great ideas and effective implementation, you inadvertently open yourself up to new perspectives.

The best way to gain an edge in the ever-changing competitive landscape is by understanding different markets, tapping into new opportunities, and devising strategies tailored to local demands. Feel free to explore different cultures!

We've all heard the saying "It takes two to tango,"[1] but I've learned that it takes a world to get the best results. No matter how different everyone may be, there's always something we can learn from each other.

The cost advantage aside, I've experienced tangible value with the work I've outsourced to different countries. There were challenges that I faced with products and campaigns that were quickly resolved by getting a broader perspective from outside of my usual circle.

On the flip side, if you're too restricted to your peers, your comfort zone is synonymous with stagnation.

The key lies in thinking beyond your preconceived notions of what's doable and seeking to work with people who can open your eyes to the world. This is what makes us all better marketers.

This intercultural exchange with people from different parts of the world has enabled me to develop a multifaceted perspective that I never even knew existed! It's not just about looking at your market and trying to build something impactful, it's about understanding different markets and building an authentic brand presence that speaks to customers everywhere.

And that is what led to my third golden nugget.

#3 Get the multigenerational mix involved

The multigenerational mix, or as I would like to call it, the *multigeneration advisory council*, is invaluable for any modern organization. By unifying different generations in a communal space, the council allows businesses to take advantage of previous generations' wisdom while also bringing younger generations' insight into their decision-making process. It's important to remember that an organization isn't made up of one person but of many different perspectives and ideas.

By bringing together people from a range of ages, backgrounds, and skill sets on a council, every decision within an organization becomes more collaborative and thought out. This multigenerational view is incredibly beneficial as seasoned professionals can recall successful methods used in past projects. At the same time, younger employees can explain the current dynamics and trends within their industry or community that could influence current decisions.

Multigeneration advisory councils can be instrumental during strategic planning sessions. With multiple viewpoints being heard and weighed accordingly, organizations would no longer be restricted by traditional top-down thinking but instead encouraged by idea-sharing between various generations resulting in more meaningful conversations that lead to long-term success both as a team unit and also as individual contributors who had helped shape the plans for company growth or development.

Overall, having a multigeneration advisory council is essential because it will allow your company to effectively capture not only present-day strategies but also find ways to stay competitive with new methods built on previous successes, along with presenting novel suggestions from various points of view. It provides members with insights into how each generation works, which will allow them to work together more cooperatively through understanding one another's methodologies better and equipping everyone on how best to tackle day-to-day challenges, whether it's devising structure training or establishing potentially profitable connections. So be sure to consider all these advantages when building yours!

Act first, optimize later

In today's digital marketing landscape, the most essential skill is thinking strategically and consistently creating engaging content. After developing a deep understanding of your audience, you must ensure that your messaging and brand identity resonate with them. Once something is created, it can be difficult to gauge its potential success—which is why "act first, optimize later" (AFOL)[2] can be an effective strategy. This involves creating a post on social media and monitoring the response—if people find it enjoyable or interesting, there will be a further social activity that could provide insights into what worked well.

The concept of AFOL is based on the speed of execution coupled with continuous monitoring until desired results are achieved. The idea behind this approach is that by acting swiftly and continuously measuring performance, marketers can quickly identify patterns indicating success or failure, allowing them to adjust until the ideal result is reached.

To effectively implement AFOL solutions, marketers must first have clear insight into various engagement channels along with continuous measurement and evaluation. Through this process, they can improve targeting initiative success rates and uncover untapped opportunities across platform frameworks they may have yet to notice. They can elevate return values by continuously adapting according to realistic insights captured at all levels of business operations.

Putting AFOL into place isn't enough—implementation needs to be undertaken thoughtfully. For AFOL strategies to be successful, marketers must begin by developing a deep understanding of their audience's needs and wants. They should also determine a clear brand identity across multiple channels and audiences to ensure campaign consistency. Finally, experimentation coupled with regular measurements of results is crucial for truly understanding what strategies are most effective for achieving success over time.

Choose social media channels wisely: When creating a post for social media channels to test your ideas, it's essential to pick the right platform. Different platforms have different audiences, so you must consider which makes sense for your brand or message. For instance, if you want a younger demographic to engage with your content, choose networks like TikTok or Instagram, which attract more millennials. Alternatively, if B2B customers are more likely to respond, then consider LinkedIn as its user base skews professional rather than casual.

Generate relevant content ideas: Coming up with fresh ideas for content is a challenge but developing unique and engaging content is possible if you try. Start by keeping up with the current trends in your industry—what topics does your audience seem to be interested in? Coming up with fresh ideas for content is a challenge but developing unique and engaging content is possible if you make an effort.

Look at what competitors are doing and get inspired by their successes: This can give you an idea of what has worked for them in the past. Then, gather data around popular topics so that when creating new posts or videos, you have evidence to support your claims. Keep an eye out for user preferences as they evolve and adjust accordingly. Finally, be creative—come up with new angles or spin on existing ideas to keep your content fresh.

As a reminder, market research is not just a phase in your project: Research and iteration should always be a part of your marketing strategy to remain successful and relevant.

Monitor your results: Social media analytics tools make it easy to monitor how well each post performs—both short term (impressions) and long term (actions). Impressions refer to clicks per hour/day, while actions relate to conversions such as purchases or followers gained over days/weeks/months, etc. It's important that after each post, you check these metrics so that better decisions can be made around future posts and overall strategy refinement. This is especially true when relying on trial-and-error techniques such as acting first/optimizing later since they depend heavily on data-driven approaches to maximize the ROI associated with each campaign cycle.

Adjust your strategy based on results: Once you have gathered enough performance data related to your posts, it's time to take actionable next steps consistent with those results—either by refining an existing idea even more or abandoning it altogether if not successful enough. Utilizing tests run like this ensures adjustments are made only after working strategies are observed while confirming value propositions are adequately met either by users individually or groups of combined followerships depending on particular model requirements. This also means making modifications rapidly based on cues from real-world feedback instead of assumptions due to quick turnaround periods required by rising consumer expectations.

AFOL solutions yield many benefits for brands, including more efficient resources and more engaged customers. These solutions can help organizations re-engage dormant stakeholders, increase conversions, and create incremental revenue streams.

Are you emotionally invested in your brand?

It makes a world of difference when you are emotionally invested in what you're doing. We've all experienced this when someone does their job, and they do exactly what they're supposed to do, nothing more, nothing less, but their heart and soul are not in it. When I think of being emotionally invested, I immediately recall my friend, Eric Tash.[3] Eric is a marketer and has had a long career in consumer packaged goods marketing. He is a connector and believes in doing well by doing good with the help of Your Brand Coach's proprietary core value system. This is the same one you did for yourself at the beginning of the book. (By the way, can you recite your core values from memory?)

Around 25 years ago, Eric's dad, an accountant, decided one morning to get up early and go to a business networking meeting to connect with other business professionals. After a few months, he noticed that he was growing his practice. Eric's father taught him, "Growth happens when we put ourselves out of our comfort zone."

Eric wanted to start a podcast but hadn't found a good reason. So, I helped him figure out why he wanted to create one, and then I provided him with a structure. For Eric, hosting and editing podcasts is an uncomfortable zone.

Watching Eric draw inspiration from his father's decision and start his venture strengthens my confidence in authentic entrepreneurs willing to learn and evolve solely for their dreams. These are the ones who can make a promise and keep it.

Eric's podcast, Worthy for Thirty, is an incredibly successful initiative he single-handedly created and brought to life.[4] His guests are all business leaders spearheading phenomenal projects or running successful ventures in their respective fields, and they share some truly inspiring stories on the podcast. Not only does this further Eric's status in the industry, it also serves as a fantastic platform of inspiration for people seeking motivation and knowledge in their entrepreneurial journey.

Eric has a passion for his work that has allowed him to grow exponentially in a relatively short period. Through his emotional investment and sense of ownership, he was able to follow through on creating 18 episodes of his podcast and decide to expand it across multiple platforms, such as live events, charitable work, and more. He realized that the only way to move forward is by instilling pride through the impression he leaves behind with each project he takes on. Eric's success story exemplifies the power of being engaged with one's work to reach new goals.

Let's get in the mix

A great disc jockey can create a miraculous experience. As they begin to play, the dance floor quickly populates, their music intensifies until it captures you, leading you to join in dancing. A similar occurrence can transpire during brand development. Recently, I was writing from what appeared to be just a coffee shop. Nonetheless, it housed a café, florist, and bar too. I wrote there between 3 pm and 5 pm, and as soon as the evening light set in, someone began placing votive lights at each table and dimming the house lights. Swiftly after that, I was ordering a Manhattan! This phenomenon is not limited to restaurants alone, it happens with advertising campaigns and branding initiatives. You become informed of a company quickly and unpretentiously; abruptly, you are more intrigued than before due to the firm's evidence of offering more value to your life. Ah, marketing! When you think like a marketer, this sentiment surfaces regardless of where you are, who you are with, and what you are doing (even when the product isn't as captivating as a café/florist/bar!). All this energy and vigor should be implemented into your work, even if the venture may not be enthralling, as mentioned before.

Do you remember the passage about critical thinking earlier on in this book? This is followed in a specific sequence. That was an effective method for me, and I am proposing it to you as a model. However, does that mean that you must go through inquiry after inquiry and address each one? Does that signify that you need to observe every step I arranged in their given order? No. Branding is fluid. The process is bespoke. Your best ideas will come when you are thinking about them the least and have less pressure, so make sure you keep a notepad with you or an app to take notes when inspiration strikes.

Marketing is an opportunity to grow, learn, and build relationships with people you admire

The marketing profession can be a difficult one to navigate. Whether creating a new strategy or trying to pitch an existing one, it can take a lot of work to make your ideas heard in an established business. But with the right approach, any marketer can successfully advocate for and implement their strategies and make their ideas a reality. And if you don't have the foundational details in your toolbox, it will be challenging to build something meaningful for yourself and your company. So be patient with yourself and ensure you are selecting a company to work with that aligns with your value system. If you are not given any autonomy, a team, a budget, or respect, or if your manager sees you and marketing as unnecessary, you may not be in a company where you can thrive or grow.

My marketing growth came from working my way up the ranks with people I liked and respected who had something to teach me. I learned from people I didn't necessarily see eye to eye with. And then some people were too short-sighted and lost my respect so early that I knew it was time for me to move on.

The most successful marketers bring knowledge and trustworthiness to the table. They've done their homework, and they understand the inner workings of the organization as well as external trends. This allows them to come forward with facts, stats, numbers, or case studies demonstrating why their idea could work—and why it's worth supporting. This gives them credibility with their colleagues and leaders, allowing them to be better prepared for any objections or questions that may arise during conversations.

Marketers must be persistent if they want to get ahead. You must stay true to your mission even if everyone in the room doesn't believe in your proposal. Whether it takes days or weeks for others to catch on, don't give up on your idea—stick by it until your vision begins taking shape.

No matter what obstacles are thrown your way, always keep sight of what you set out to achieve in the first place. In some cases, you may have to compromise but never give up fully—keep pushing forward until your mission is complete!

Getting your feet wet on a campaign is a great way to learn how to create your movement and make an impact. It gives you hands-on experience with the day-to-day work it takes to make a successful campaign, from organizing volunteers and fundraising to engaging with voters and handling communication tactics. It also allows you to gain insight into the challenges of campaigning and gain a better understanding of the resources needed to succeed.

Meaningful marketers take a holistic approach to their work, combining creative, technological, and analytical skills to create meaningful stories and content that resonate with their audience. They focus on building relationships and trust with customers, prospects, partners, and influencers by providing value through helpful content and personalized outreach. A purposeful marketer understands the big picture of their overall marketing strategy and the granular aspects of the customer journey.

Meaningful marketers have a service mindset because they understand that people are behind every marketing message. They put time into getting to know their audience deeper so they can create relevant and timely offerings, not just messaging, which will generate interest, engagement, and sales.

Overall, a modern-day purposeful marketer emphasizes quality over quantity when it comes to content creation and customer interactions, striving for continuous improvement at every stage of the process to deliver measurable results while maintaining integrity throughout.

Do you have what it takes to be a meaningful brand builder?

Brand purpose can empower your audience, but the actions of a brand need to be consistent with this purpose. Showing customers, rather than just telling them, the type of empowerment available helps them better understand it. After all, when the hard work is done, and your marketing team is ready to set the plan into motion with the campaign, and corresponding messaging, companies may find that anyone can use them. So, one thing to consider is the reason for alignment. Think about it this way: does what you're doing as a company have the same impact if you take your company name out of the content? Often, it does not.

I have worked on numerous projects where we have gone through a process of strategy building, studying research, and defining a specific audience. Then one of the first proposed solutions is something like "we empower you!" or another generic statement. When marketers say things like this, it reveals how little connection and understanding they share with their audience and what they want or need. It also discounts marketers and their strategic contributions as the result of a months-long strategic endeavor that leads to a conclusion that a person with no knowledge of any research can come up with.

Exhibit the meaningful marketer mindset

Today, successful companies understand that the most important drivers of success and customer loyalty are not low prices but rather brands that connect to the hearts and minds of their customers. Brand valuations give companies a blueprint for maximizing interactions with their customers. By connecting your company's brand values to its performance, you can ensure long-term customer loyalty and engagement. Here is a list of value-oriented attributes that encapsulate what it's like to be a modern-day marketer and brand builder:

- Being simple
- Thinking at scale
- Staying nimble
- Being curious
- Following a methodical approach
- Applying analytical thinking
- Being clever
- Achieving results-oriented outcomes

Being simple: Keep your message clear and conversational

Crafting content for digital channels requires simplicity to keep the message clear. By avoiding jargon and spelling out possibly confusing concepts, you can ensure that readers understand your ideas as clearly as possible. Additionally, writing shorter sentences will help your audience grasp your ideas more quickly. The fast-paced environment of today's world means that keeping things simple is necessary to be successful. Streamlining processes and making decisions quickly while maintaining quality will enable you to find solutions efficiently and effectively.

Thinking at scale: Automate when possible

Investing in automation technology can help companies quickly and easily scale up operations cost-effectively. Automation processes, such as project management software and artificial intelligence, can help streamline complex projects or tasks, freeing up company resources for other important tasks. Additionally, it is essential to focus on tasks that capitalize on strengths and cut down or eliminate any excesses to ensure maximum efficiency and maximize value for the organization. Automation is an excellent tool for scaling operations quickly and efficiently without going over budget.

Staying nimble: Be prepared to pivot quickly

In today's rapidly changing digital market landscape, being nimble is a must for staying ahead of customer demands and competition. Being able to react quickly to customer feedback or emerging trends is essential for any successful marketing plan, so make sure that flexibility remains front of mind even during planning stages!

Being curious: Harnessing the power of curiosity and creativity to create something as unique as you are

To stay ahead of the competition, it is important to be bold and ask questions and seek answers. It is essential to tap into the "curious mindset" that can lead you to uncover valuable insights, new ideas, and fast solutions to help make your brand stand out from the rest. Being curious encourages exploration and helps build a more creative approach when developing your brand. Not only does this promote growth for your brand but being curious about different trends can also help keep your team up to date on industry news and insights.

Methodical approach: Always follow through on goals you set out to achieve

Setting out goals before commencing any task is paramount to ensuring success. When tackling complex problems, these goals can be broken down into smaller achievable objectives to make the overwhelming task more manageable and less daunting. Methodical execution plans that focus on outcomes should be established to ensure progress is consistent and well-paced throughout the process. Additionally, monitored progress needs to be measured through measurable metrics so the effectiveness of strategies can be monitored and optimized accordingly when needed; this will enable a proper assessment of whether or not a particular decision or solution yielded satisfactory results for the organization. Out-of-the-box and creative thinking is also required to stay ahead of competitors in a competitive market that changes quickly.

Analytical thinking: Pay attention to the metrics that matter most

Data is a powerful tool for marketers and digital professionals. Keeping up with all the different data sources available and cultivating actionable insights from them can feel like a full-time job. That's where precision analytics comes in. By focusing on relevant data across touchpoints, time zones, platforms, and other factors, you can create reports that not only give you an understanding of how users engage with your content but also provide insights into how these behaviors unfold over time. With this data, you can better target your efforts for optimization, lead generation, and other activities. Ultimately, precise analysis of this data helps you make informed decisions regarding strategies and plans, so your business always has the edge over the competition.

Being clever: Stand out, make an impression

It is essential to be clever in your brand marketing to stand out from the competition, create a memorable impression on potential customers, and make them more likely to become loyal. Clever brand marketing can also help generate awareness of your product or service, attract attention to your message, and communicate more engagingly with more significant benefits.

Results-oriented: Focus on the outcomes more than the inputs

Having a results-oriented focus for any organization or individual project is necessary to track progress and identify areas for improvement. Using specific campaigns with an overarching goal helps you measure your progress and adjust accordingly. Additionally, creating content targeting the proper demographic will increase conversions more efficiently than a generic approach. Focusing on consistent campaigns over time allows you to optimize future initiatives, resulting in increased ROI. Together, these practices help ensure that everyone's efforts are going towards reaching successful objectives and ultimately attaining success.

Join the Meaningful Marketer Movement

Are you looking for an opportunity to become part of something meaningful? If so, the Meaningful Marker Movement may be right for you. This movement is based on ethical strategies that can be applied in individual lives or businesses to create positive outcomes; in other words, everything you learned in this book. You will gain access to a wealth of information and resources that can help you make real changes and improvements and meet like-minded people working through the same issues as you. Visit jaymandel.com for more information about joining the Meaningful Marker Movement and using these strategies to your advantage today.

I am championing the cause of creating more diversity and inclusion in the workplace, particularly with new generations who often bring valuable perspectives to the table. Together with this movement and platform, we will consistently share stories and advice on how people can develop their self-confidence and better connect with themselves and those around them.

I am boldly committing to eliminating systemic inequality in all forms, enabling many talented individuals to secure rewarding roles across various industries. My goal is to help you see that everyone has something valuable to contribute and remind businesses everywhere that it pays to nurture their biggest asset—their staff.

As a part of the Meaningful Marketing Movement, the multigenerational advisory council will bring far more than just having a diverse group of minds to the company. Given that there's no one right answer in business today, having an outside perspective from a different pool of individuals can help businesses stay competitive in their respective markets while developing more creative solutions to real-world problems. A multigenerational council can also provide insight into how to better utilize existing resources, such as technology and marketing platforms, by considering the individual demands of each generation. To ensure success with this type of initiative, you will need to establish clear guidelines and criteria for the types of people you are looking for to make sure they complement existing staff and provide fresh ideas that benefit not only their business but society as a whole.

Have you ever wondered why some marketers get better results than others? Join the Meaningful Marketer Movement to gain access to "The Mind of a Marketer," an exploration into a marketer's brain and why certain marketing tactics succeed (and others don't).

As a knowledgeable marketer, I will uncover my insights on efficiently publicizing your offering or service in an epoch of social media, where detaching oneself from the competition is crucial. You'll gain from unprecedented plans and ingenious answers that will support you in reaching your audience through imaginative means that few have considered. Visit jaymandel.com to learn more.

Building brands with passion takes time. Be patient

Developing and sustaining a successful brand takes extensive planning, research, and dedication. It is essential to keep up with marketing trends to remain relevant in the digital world and adjust branding strategies when necessary. Additionally, consistent communication with customers through both words and actions should be implemented for the growth of the business to take hold. Although a lot of time and effort goes into creating a successful brand, it pays off in the long run when businesses experience better reputations, enhanced customer loyalty, higher brand awareness, etc. With patience comes success, as when it comes down to it, establishing a powerful brand is no different from planting a tree—you can't expect rapid progress. Still, you must nurture it over time if you want to witness impressive results.

Endnotes

1 *Cambridge Dictionary* [online] (nd) "it takes two to tango," dictionary. cambridge.org/dictionary/english/it-takes-two-to-tango (archived at https://perma.cc/96P5-LA82)

2 Parks, B (2021, July 29) A mantra for early-stage SAAS startups, Baremetrics, baremetrics.com/blog/a-mantra-for-early-stage-saas-startups (archived at https://perma.cc/KC36-P3KW)

3 Mandel, J (2022, November 5) Interview with Eric Tash. Used with permission

4 Tash, E (nd) Worthy for Thirty, Podcast, Substack, worthyforthirty.substack. com/ (archived at https://perma.cc/9Q62-DXXU)

INDEX

From 4 December 2025 the EU Responsible Person (GPSR) is:
eucomply oÜ, Pärnu mnt. 139b – 14, 11317 Tallinn, Estonia
www.eucompliancepartner.com

www.ingramcontent.com/pod-product-compliance
Lightning Source LLC
Chambersburg PA
CBHW041208220326
41597CB00030BA/5100

9 781398 609792